```
KF          Menendez, Albert J.
4865
.M46        The December wars.
1993


$19.95
```

DATE			
AUG 2 0 1994			

BAKER & TAYLOR BOOKS

The December Wars

Religious Symbols
and Ceremonies
in the Public Square

Albert J. Menendez

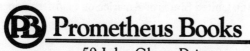

Prometheus Books
59 John Glenn Drive
Buffalo, New York 14228-2197

Published 1993 by Prometheus Books

97 96 95 94 93   5 4 3 2 1

Library of Congress Cataloging-in-Publication Data

Menendez, Albert J.
    The December Wars : religious symbols and ceremonies in the
public square / Albert J. Menendez.
        p.   cm.
    Includes bibliographical references and index.
    ISBN 0-87975-857-0
    1. Church and state—United States. 2. Christmas—United States.
3. Church and state—History. I. Title.
KF4865.M46   1993
323.44′2—dc20   93-5591
                           R060bb 03933   CIP

Published in cooperation with Americans for Religious Liberty, P.O. Box 6656, Silver Spring, Maryland 20916. Americans for Religious Liberty (ARL) is a nonprofit public interest educational organization, founded in 1981, dedicated to preserving the American tradition of religious intellectual, and personal freedom in a pluralistic secular democratic state. Membership is open to all who share that purpose. ARL publishes a newsletter and other material, operates a speakers bureau, and has been involved in litigation in defense of separation of church and state and freedom of conscience. Inquiries are welcome.

For Shirley

Contents

Contents

Acknowledgments

I am especially grateful for the superb assistance from Marie Gore, who used her computer skills to help shape the manuscript at every stage. I appreciate the advice, prodding, and intellectual challenges that my colleague, Edd Doerr, always brings to projects like this, and I am appreciative of the assistance provided by Marc Stern and Ronald Lindsay.

Introduction

Christmas has always been controversial. It may be a season of unalloyed joy to many if not most people, or at least a time of friendship, festivity and good food. It may also be a time of conflict, of unfulfilled expectations and enhanced sorrow as the inequalities of life are made more pronounced or manifest.

It is also a time no one can ignore try as hard as some might. It is the commercial season par excellence, the do or die time for many business enterprises, and a season with its own panoply of music and literature. It is a time of tradition, sentiment, renewal, and continuity. It is a time of universality despite real and significant religious differences that underline the celebratory nature of it all.

As this book will show, the season and festival of Christmas has always been divisive and complicated. The legal hassles and commercial conflicts of the past decades in the United States are not anomalies. They are not the result of mean-spirited atheist Grinches who are trying to steal Christmas from God-fearing patriotic Americans. They represent only the latest chapter in a long story of conflict about the nature and meaning of Christmas, a conflict dating all the way back to the fourth century.

There are sincere and principled people on both sides of the

11

Christmas controversy, who differ strongly in what they believe should be the appropriate role of government in celebrating or in mandating the celebration of a religious holiday in an officially secular state.

Christmas has become not only a big business but a world wide production encompassing the majority of nations. Of the world's 200 countries, 151 observe Christmas as a legal holiday on the 25th of December. While most of the 151 are predominantly Christian, many Christmas-observing nations are non-Christian. Muslim countries like Bangladesh, Indonesia, Jordan, Pakistan, Sudan, and Syria observe Christmas as legal or banking holidays. So do religiously mixed nations like India, Brunei, Malaysia, Sri Lanka, and Singapore. The strongly Buddhist Union of Myanmar (formerly Burma) observes Christmas, as does South Korea. Three Eastern Orthodox nations (Cyprus, Bulgaria and Rumania) celebrate Christmas on December 25 rather than January 7. Belarus observes both December 25 and January 7 as Christmas holidays.

Ten countries where Eastern or Coptic Orthodoxy predominates celebrate Christmas on January 7. Armenia celebrates it on January 6, the western Epiphany. Called Armenian Christmas Day, it is really an Epiphany festival.

Four African nations which have undergone Marxist-oriented revolutions observe December 25 as a secular holiday. Angola, Mozambique and Sao Tome and Principe call it Family Day, while the People's Republic of Congo calls the holiday Children's Day.

Thirty-four other nations do not celebrate Christmas as a legal holiday. Most are countries where Islam is the state religion. A few have Communist governments, e.g., China and Cuba. Hindu Nepal, Buddhist Thailand and the Jewish state of Israel also, not unexpectedly, have no Christmas holiday. This is also true for Japan, where Buddhism and Shintoism have shaped the culture.

Twenty-one nations of the world observe Epiphany as a legal or banking holiday. Seventeen of them observe January 6, the Western date for the observance. Included are several predominantly Catholic countries like Austria, Italy, and Spain, several

Eastern Orthodox ones like Greece and Cyprus, Lutheran Finland and Sweden, and religiously mixed Germany and Switzerland. The Virgin Islands calls the holiday Three Kings Day. Two Catholic countries, Colombia and Venezuela, observe the holiday on the Monday following January 6, while Eastern Orthodox Ethiopia and Georgia celebrate it on January 19 according to the Julian Calendar.[1]

This story begins in a world far different from that of America in 1993. It begins in Rome and the outermost regions of its Empire in a time when a long-persecuted religion suddenly emerged from repression to begin a restructuring of the world. This fourth century emergence of Christianity and its rapid establishment as the dominant religion of the western world brought immense changes to everyday life.

The development of Christmas and other days and seasons deemed sacred and holy, and the intermingling between Christian and pagan cultures are the subjects of this book's two opening chapters. They are followed in chapter three by the story of how the Reformation, and the Puritan and Victorian eras in England modified and reshaped the interplay of religion, folklore and public life.

In the fourth chapter a brief history of the role of Christmas in the public life of the United States is the focus. This historical reference point leads into the role of the American presidency, commercial interests and civic group promoters of ever-more elaborate and politically prominent Christmas celebrations.

The sixth chapter describes the contentious problems of religious holidays, devotional activities, and the differing expectations of America's religious groups when the public schools are in the crossfire of the Christmas and Hanukkah seasons.

The seventh chapter surveys the complex legal tangles that these controversies have engendered, from local councils to the United States Supreme Court itself. A thorough review of the legal literature brings the reader to the final chapter, which explores the implications of this issue for church-state relations in the last decade of this century. The final chapter summarizes the broad implications of this issue of religious ceremonies and symbols in the public square, looks at the players and their roles, and ponders the future of church-state separation and the framework of religious pluralism in our nation.

Notes

1. See *World Holiday and Time Guide 1993* (New York: J. P. Morgan and Co., Inc., 1992).

1

The Origins and Development of Christmas

Why has Christmas been celebrated on December 25 since the fourth century, and is it really the day on which Jesus was born? Neither question can be answered with certitude but the two are inextricably linked.

Some historians argue that Christian theologians of the early fourth century tried to calculate the exact birth of Jesus by accepting an early tradition that John the Baptist was born at the autumn equinox, September 25. Since the Gospels claim that Jesus was conceived exactly six months after John, the date of March 25 was established and celebrated as the Annunciation of Mary. Therefore, nine months later, December 25, was calculated as the probable date of the birth of Jesus. Franciscan scholar Berard Doerger describes the development of this theory:

> It is said that this coincidence of Christ's birth with the winter solstice would have been considered by theologians and the Christian people in general at that time as an enchanting work of divine providence. The idea that Jesus was born into the world just on the day that the sun was being born again and

overcoming the night was an idea freighted with great symbolism and one that could exalt the hearts of all.[1]

Doerger admits that another explanation holds more historical weight.

The stronger argument for the establishment of the feast of Christmas on December 25th is that the Church authorities did choose that day because it was a pagan feast to the Unconquered Sun-God (Sol invictus). The Roman Emperor Aurelian had established this feast on December 25th throughout the empire in A.D. 247, hoping that this feast would help unite and strengthen his vast empire.[2]

Therefore, the Church at Rome would be able to counter the civil celebration and "immunize Christians against the attraction of the pagan elements of the feast."[3] Doerger also suggests that "the symbolism of the 'Unconquerable Sun' renewing itself and overcoming the darkness at the time of the winter solstice does contain much food for poetry and reflection in relation to Christ's birth."[4]

By no means did the Roman Church's decision to celebrate December 25 as the birthday of Jesus settle the issue for all Christians. St. Clement of Alexandria wrote that many of his third century contemporaries regarded May 20 as the day of Christ's birth, while others preferred the sixth or tenth of January. Clement himself opted for the 18th of November. St. Cyprian, a century later, thought March 28 was the correct date while St. Epiphanias of Cyprus argued strenuously for January 6, the date which soon came to be celebrated in the Eastern churches as Epiphany. Still others argued for March 25. St. Hippolytus made the strongest argument for December 25.[5] One eighteenth century Jesuit, Antonio Lupi, observed that there is not a single month of the year to which the Nativity has not been assigned.[6]

Another contributory factor to the selection of December 25 was the existence of Bacchanalian festivities honoring the god

Saturn, and called Saturnalia, which were held from the seventeenth to the twenty-third of December. The emerging Christian leadership sought to counteract these rites with distinctively Christian ones.

Christian liturgists and poets now called Jesus "The sun of Righteousness," "the sun of Justice," "the light of the world," and "the true light, which enlightens everyone," echoing John's Gospel and the Jewish prophet Malachi.

It should be noted that the celebration of Christmas as a separate holy day for the Nativity of Christ developed in the Western, or Roman church, apart from the earlier feast of the Epiphany, which originated in the East in the late second or early third centuries.

The sixth of January was the birthday of Aeon, the god of time and eternity in Greco-Roman religion. Eastern Christians sought to counter this celebration with a feast of their own, which emphasized the "manifestation" or "showing forth" of Christ to the world. At this time the only other holy days celebrated in the various Christian communities were Easter, and possibly, Pentecost, fifty days later. St. Clement of Alexandria mentions Epiphany in his early third century writings, as do his contemporaries St. Hippolytus of Rome and St. Gregory the Wonderworker. A fourth century Eastern Christian document, "The Apostolic Constitution," mentions Epiphany, as do St. John Chrysostom and St. Augustine.[7]

One fourth-century church father, Epiphanias, suggested that the Epiphany feast may have originated among Egyptian Gnostics, who spent the night of January 5-6 in singing, flute-playing and other ceremonies in honor of Kore, a virgin maiden who gave birth to Aeon. These nocturnal ceremonies were accompanied by candlelight. Other scholars have traced Epiphany to the unorthodox Basilidian movement of the second century.[8]

Many Eastern Orthodox and Eastern-Rite Catholics prefer the term "Theophany" to Epiphany, because it implies that Christ was divine. Theophany refers to the showing forth of Jesus in his divine nature, they say, while Epiphany refers to his appearance in human form. In the East, Epiphany, still one of the twelve major holy days, commemorated the birth of Christ, his baptism, his first miracle at Cana in Galilee, and the homage of the Wise Men or Magi. It was an all-inclusive feast day. But because of the desire of Western Church authorities to counter the *Sol invictus* and Saturnalia celebrations, Epiphany was gradually separated from Christmas.

East and West did something of a swap. Epiphany spread to the West as a separate January 6 celebration in the mid-fourth century. It was celebrated in Gaul by 361, in northern Italy and Spain by 383 and in northern Africa by the year 400. This feast became a state holiday during the reign of Theodosius in 438.[9]

Meanwhile, the Western church was vigorously promoting its separate feast day for the Nativity of Christ, called *Nativitas Domini*. The first historical reference to Christmas comes in a document called the *Depositio Martyrum*, dating from around 335–336. This was an early calendar of the saints and martyrs commemorated by the Church in Rome, a custom dating from the second century. This increasingly popular tradition of compiling biographical information about heroes, martyrs, confessors and others who suffered persecution for their faith under the Roman Imperial authorities led to a cult of saints.[10] Ukrainian Catholic scholar Julian Katrij explains the significance of these events:

> The feast of the Nativity of our Lord was first separated from the Theophany in the Roman Church, which under Pope Julius I (337–352), began to celebrate the Nativity of Christ on the 25th of December. The chronographic collection of calendars up to the year 354, which bears different names but is known by the name of the Calendar of Furius Philocalus, the chapter dealing with the dates of the death of the Martyrs, under the 25th of December, states: "The Day of the Nativity of Christ in Bethlehem." And in another chapter there is the note: "During the consuls of Caesar Augustus and Emilius Paulus, Christ was born on the 25th of December on Friday, on the 15th day of the new moon."[11]

The Roman Church promoted the Nativity celebration with the zeal of a convert. Church leaders commissioned separate liturgies and increasingly complex and elaborate ceremonies to honor a day which commemorated the Incarnation of the Son of God. Theology was linked to celebration, as the increasingly dominant and influential bishops and theologians sought to convince the larger secular world of the truth and orthodoxy of their interpretations of the message announced by Jesus. Western church leaders sought to defend the doctrine of the Incarnation by amassing evidence and incorporating it into the liturgy. Julian Katrij describes the process:

> In the first centuries the Church, especially the Western Church, blended not only the Nativity of our Lord and His Baptism with the Theophany, but also the homage of the Three Magi, the miracle in Cana of Galilee, the miracle of the multiplication of the loaves, and in some places even the resurrection of Lazarus, because all these events bore testimony to the Theophany, the manifestations of God on earth. This celebration of several events from the life of Jesus Christ together with the feast of the Theophany was one of the chief reasons why the Western Church was the first to separate the feast of the Nativity of our Lord from the feast of the Theophany and why it began to celebrate this feast on a separate day.[12]

Sermons by eloquent preachers echoed throughout the realm, promoting the uniqueness of the Christmas feast. Zenon of Verona, in the early fourth century, is believed to have delivered the first Christmas sermon.[13] Sermons of these orators are still extant, as are the Christmas homilies of St. Augustine and St. Ephrem the Syrian. Hymns and poems extolling the Christmas feast soon appeared.[14] Eventually, the ancient bishoprics of Alexandria (in 431) and Jerusalem followed the pattern now established, even though Epiphany remained a popular and sentimental feast day, replete as it was with imagery and theological subtlety. Epiphany remained an important day for the baptism of converts (called catechumens), as did Holy Saturday, the Eve of Easter. There was one holdout: the Armenian Orthodox Church refused to establish a separate Christmas feast, and still celebrates the Nativity as part of the Epiphany.[15]

Two additional events strengthened and ratified the Christmas holiday. In the fourth century, St. Helena, mother of the first Christian emperor, Constantine, claimed to have discovered the actual birth site of Jesus in Bethlehem. Her enthusiasm for the "Holy Places" and relics in the Holy Land promoted a new tourism industry for prosperous Christians who wished to visit the sacred sites of their faith's origins. Under Helena's influence an important pilgrimage church was erected on the alleged site of the Nativity in Bethlehem, where to this day the Latin Patriarch of Jerusalem celebrates midnight Mass each Christmas Eve.

Perhaps more important was the declaration of Christmas as a legal holiday throughout the Roman Empire by Emperor Theodosius in his codex of laws in 438. Emperor Justinian reaffirmed Christmas as an official state holiday in his law code of 535.[16] Theodosius also forbade games in the circus on Sunday in his February 1, 425 edict. Earlier Emperors Honorius and Arcadius forbade the circus on Christmas, Epiphany and Eastertide.[17]

The German church historian Kellner observes, "The legislation concerning Christmas and Epiphany exhibits a good deal of vacillation, probably connected with the fact that these two festivals were not yet generally celebrated and recognized everywhere in the fourth century."[18] Emperor Justinian moved further toward official recognition of Christmas when he ruled in the early fifth century that the law courts would not sit on Christmas or Epiphany.[19]

As can be seen, there was an important connection between the development of a Christian calendar of holy days and observances, related to the concept of a sanctification of time, and closer church-state relationships with an increasingly Christianized government. Kellner also reminds us of one other significant point: "The Church's year is built upon a single basis and according to one plan, which did not originate in the mind of any one person, but developed out of the historical conditions resulting from the connection of Christianity with Judaism."[20]

Kellner is also quite emphatic that the promotion of a separate Nativity festival was part and parcel of the Catholic and Orthodox drive for superiority over rival Christians, such as the Arians and Donatists, who did not favor the theology or the propriety of the feast. Here is how Kellner describes the politics of Christmas promotion in Constantinople:

> The second capital of the empire had long been a stronghold of Arianism, so that the Orthodox had dwindled down to a mere handful, and no longer possessed a church of their own in the city. During this period Christmas was certainly not celebrated in Constantinople. Not till after the death of Valens, and the elevation of Theodosius the Great (19th January 379) did the Catholics breathe freely once more. They received as bishop Gregory of Nazianzus, who began his labors as a stranger and sojourner in a small private chapel which he called the Anastasia. Here, on the 25th of December in 379 or 380, Christmas was celebrated for the first time in Constantinople. Thus one of the first acts of the restorer of Catholicism in the capital was the introduction of the new festival.[21]

It is clearly evident that superior eloquence by numerous church fathers and a planned promotion of doctrinal orthodoxy were central to the triumph of Christmas at this crucial juncture in church history. Again, Kellner is forthright: "We see that it was no mere accident that Christmas began to be celebrated in the East just at this particular period. It was the moment when Catholics began successfully to repel Arianism. It was those who attacked Arianism with most vigor and success who promoted the spread of the new festival in the East."[22]

The Christmas festival soon became more and more important in the church calendar. It as assigned an octave, an eightday period of worship and celebration culminating in the Feast of the Circumcision on January 1. The octave originated in Judaism, and was adopted by Christians. Easter and Epiphany were honored by octaves before the eighth century, and it was inevitable that Christmas would be provided with one also. In addition, the first day of January had become a popular secular holiday, given to popular dances, masquerades and entertainments. Church authorities sought to counter this trend as early as the seventh century. Church councils in France and Spain condemned the secular festivities and began to make the Circumcision a holy day of obligation.[23]

New Year's Day has always had the character of a festive day, a new beginning as it were. Julius Caesar shifted the beginning of the new year from March 1 to January 1 in 46 B.C.[24]

In the sixth century arose the custom of the Three Low Masses (immortalized in a famous and frequently anthologized short story by Alphonse Daudet). This was a special privilege accorded to the clergy and reveals something of the increasing prominence and popularity of the Christmas holiday. Doerger describes the evolution of this custom:

Since the sixth century every priest was permitted to celebrate three Masses on Christmas, which custom continues in our day. There are special Mass texts and readings for a midnight Mass, a Mass at dawn, and a Mass during the day.

The origin of these three Masses is of historical nature and developed in Rome. At first, in the fourth century, there was only one Mass, celebrated by the Pope at St. Peter's in the morning about nine o'clock. Then in the fifth century, the midnight Mass and an early morning Mass were added in imitation of the Jerusalem Christians, who were already celebrating Mass at two different times on Christmas. The Jerusalem Christians would celebrate a midnight Mass in the Church which Emperor Constantine had built over the cave of Christ's birth in Bethlehem; then they would return in procession to Jerusalem and celebrate another Mass in the early morning there. In Rome the midnight Mass was celebrated in the Crib Church of St. Mary Major; the second Mass, in the

Church of the Resurrection of St. Anastasius; and the third Mass, in St. Peter's. From Rome the custom of the three Masses on Christmas spread throughout the western Church.[25]

Another extension of the preeminence of Christmas was the development of Advent as a season of preparation and penitence. A fifth century French bishop, Perpetuus of Tours, is credited with the first observance of Advent. Official sources in the sixth century also show that the Advent season had become a firmly established practice. Its duration varied, from as early as St. Martin's Day (November 11) to as late as four Sundays preceding Christmas, the present pattern in the Western church. Advent was observed in Rome at the time of Pope Gregory the Great, and it was clearly celebrated in Gaul, Spain, Egypt, and Milan somewhat earlier. Advent is not mentioned in the homilies of St. Augustine and Leo I, so its origin belongs to a later period.[26]

Christmas also gave birth to a series of somewhat-related holidays during the twelve days between December 25 and January 6. The day after Christmas was appointed as the feast of St. Stephen, the Protomartyr, while St. John the Evangelist received the next day. The Feast of the Holy Innocents, a grim reminder of King Herod's alleged slaughter of all male children under age 2, is celebrated on the 28th of December. The Feast of the Holy Family is observed on the Sunday within the octave of Christmas. Since the Second Vatican Council, the Feast of the Circumcision on New Years Day has become the Solemnity of Mary, the Mother of God, allegedly an older holiday.[27]

As Christmas became more prolonged as a season rather than a single holy day, one additional feast day, borrowed somewhat from Judaism, became the final gasp of the celebratory period. Since the fourth century, February 2nd has been observed as the feast of the Presentation of Christ in the Temple, also called the Purification of the Blessed Virgin Mary, the only church holiday with alternate names and focuses. (It also has a third name, Candlemas, in observance of the candlelight processions and light motifs associated with the early liturgy.) Based on events related to Luke's gospel, the Purification was first observed in Jerusalem. The Emperor Justinian ordered the feast's celebration throughout the Byzantine Empire in 542. It spread to Rome in the late seventh century and to Spain and France a few years later.

According to Egeria, a Spanish lady of means who may be said to have inaugurated the concept of religious pilgrimages during a late fourth century visit to the Holy Places in Jerusalem, this feast day was well established by the 380s.[28]

Not all Christians approved of the Candlemas feast. Tertullian and Lactantius objected to it because of its similarity to a pre-Christian festival called Lupercalia, during which torches and candles were paraded about in honor of Ceres and Proserpine.[29] Defenders contended that it was quite a biblical occasion, commemorating as it does the appearances of Jesus and Mary in the Temple forty days after his birth. The feast remained widely popular in the West, and the Church of England retained it as a Prayer Book holy day, though some of its external observances were discontinued in 1548.[30]

Notes

1. Berard T. Doerger, *I Am With You Always: Reflections on the Church Year* (Huntington, Ind.: Our Sunday Visitor, 1988), pp. 37–39.

2. Ibid., p. 39.

3. Ibid.

4. Ibid.

5. Julian J. Katrij, *A Byzantine Rite Liturgical Year* (Detroit: Basilian, 1983), pp. 294–95.

6. Clement A. Miles, *Christmas in Ritual and Tradition, Christian and Pagan* (London: T. Fisher Unwin, 1912), p. 23.

7. Ibid., pp. 344–46.

8. Miles, p. 21.

9. Ibid., p. 345.

10. Charles K. Riepe, *Living the Christian Seasons* (New York:

Herder and Herder, 1964), p. 22.

11. Katrij, pp. 292–93.

12. Ibid., p. 292.

13. Ibid., pp. 295–305.

14. See Matthew Britt, *Hymns of the Breviary and Missal* (New York: Benziger, 1922).

15. Katrij, pp. 295–97.

16. Ibid., p. 297.

17. K. A. Heinrich Kellner, *Heortology: A History of the Christian Festivals* (London: Kegan Paul, 1908), pp. 19, 450.

18. Kelllner, p. 18.

19. Ibid.

20. Ibid, p. 3.

21. Ibid., p. 130.

22. Ibid., p. 134.

23. Ibid., p. 164.

24. Doerger, p. 50.

25. Ibid., pp. 45–46.

26. Kellner, pp. 158–65.

27. Doerger, pp. 47–50.

28. John Wilkinson, trans. *Egeria's Travels* (London: S.P.C.K., 1971), pp. 144–46.

29. T. G. Crippen, *Christmas and Christmas Lore* (London: Blackie, 1923), p. 205.

30. Ibid., pp. 206–207.

2

Borrowing from the Past

Many ancient cultures and religious traditions considered trees to be endowed with sacred qualities. Evergreen trees, in particular, suggest eternal life and the enduring freshness of youth. Certain tree festivals seem inextricably linked to winter ceremonies which celebrated the shift away from the darkness and cold of the winter months toward the light, warmth and lengthening days of spring.

Jack Maguire places the Christmas tree evolution in this context. "The Christmas tree is the product of over 4,000 years of complex artistic, religious, political, and social input. In every period in recorded history, and in virtually every inhabited region of the globe, trees in general, and evergreen trees in particular, have been the focal point of winter ceremonies honoring the renewal of the natural world, and the refreshing of the human spirit."[1]

The Greeks held a solstice festival celebrating the defeat of Chronos by Zeus in an ancient duel of the Gods. Special trees, often evergreens, were dressed with flowers and herbs to honor Zeus's victory.

Chronos, or Saturn in the Roman religious mythology, fled to what is now Italy and brought a kind of golden age to the people. It was in honor of Saturn that a week-long festival called

Saturnalia was held, a time of feasting, revelry, gift-giving and general merriment.

Saturnalia was also a time of storytelling, of poetry and song. The evergreen was the motif of choice, as public buildings and private homes throughout the Empire were decorated with trees and boughs, topped often with candles, and small gifts. The god of wine and greenery, Bacchus, was honored with clay figurines that bore his likeness. The poet Virgil describes these scenes in his classic *Georgics*.

Saturnalia was a religious and a secular occasion, the religious aspects being observed on the opening day, December 17.

The festal customs endured through the 23rd of December. The Roman writer Lucian records the laws promulgated by the state in celebration of Saturnalia.

> All business, be it public or private, is forbidden during the feast days, save such as tends to sport and solace and delight. Let none follow their avocations saving cooks and bakers.
>
> All men shall be equal, slave and free, rich and poor, one with another.
>
> Anger, resentment, threats, are contrary to law.
>
> No discourse shall be either composed or delivered, except it be witty and lusty, conducing to mirth and jollity.[2]

On the 22nd of December, a feast of dolls called *sigillaria*, was held, during which earthenware dolls and toys were given to children. It bears a striking resemblance to the *Christkindlmarts* held in Germany and Austria today, and to the Christmas Fair held each year at the Piazza Navonna in Rome.

Saturnalia was quickly followed by another festival honoring the Kalends, the new year. This festival seems to have taken on an even rowdier demeanor than Saturnalia. Libanius, a Greek sophist of the fourth century, describes the Kalends in this way:

> The festival of the Kalends is celebrated everywhere as far as the limits of the Roman Empire extended. . . . Everywhere may

be seen carousals and well-laden tables; luxurious abundance is found in the houses of the rich, but also in the houses of the poor better food than usual is put upon the table. The impulse to spend seizes everyone. He who the whole year through has taken pleasure in saving and piling up his pence, becomes suddenly extravagant. He who erstwhile was accustomed and preferred to live poorly, now at this feast enjoys himself as much as his means will allow. . . . People are not only generous towards themselves, but also towards their fellow-men. A stream of presents pours itself out on all sides. . . . The high-roads and footpaths are covered with whole processions of laden men and beasts. . . . As the thousand flowers which burst forth everywhere are the adornment of Spring, so are the thousand presents poured out on all sides, the decoration of the Kalends feast. It may justly be said that it is the fairest time of the year. . . . The Kalends festival banishes all that is connected with toil, and allows men to give themselves up to undisturbed enjoyment. From the minds of young people it removes two kinds of dread: the dread of the schoolmaster and the dread of the stern pedagogue. The slave also it allows, so far as possible, to breathe the air of freedom. . . . Another great quality of the festival is that it teaches men not to hold too fast to their money, but to part with it and let it pass into other hands.[3]

The Roman New Year's Day was also a political occasion, during which new consuls were inducted into office. All public buildings were decorated with greenery and lights. Solemn wishes of prosperity were freely given, as were presents.

It is of some interest that the term Kalendae was adopted by the Slavic language groups as a term to describe the entire Christmas season. The Poles refer to Kolenda, the Czechs, Koleda, the Lithuanians, Kalledos, and the Russians, Kolyada, as their points of reference.[4]

Persian religion also featured a sun god named Mithra. His enthusiastic followers spread the message of his resurrection on the winter solstice, claiming that everlasting life would be granted to his devotees. His birthday, called Bramalia, seems to have been engrafted into the Saturnalia activities.

Mithraism, which originated in Persia, was a religious movement centered on Mithra, the god of contracts, the guardian of truth and the judge of souls at death. It was affirmed by believers that Mithra would come again at the end of this world to destroy the wicked with fire and to save the righteous. He became central to the rituals of Zoroastrianism, an example of the many historic mergings and borrowings between religions.

Mithraism entered the Roman Empire about sixty years before the birth of Jesus and became popular among soldiers. "It was an exclusively male cult," and promised immortality to its followers, who engaged in a kind of ritual meal including bread and wine.[5]

Clement A. Miles also notes that "Mithraism resembled Christianity in its monotheistic tendencies, its sacraments, its comparatively high morality, its doctrine of an Intercessor and Redeemer, and its vivid belief in a future life and judgment to come. Moreover, Sunday was its holy-day dedicated to the Sun."[6]

In the cold climes of Northern Europe, trees were venerated for their essential character in providing shelter and fuel. Evergreen and oak trees played leading roles in religious rites adopted by the various indigenous peoples who inhabited the vast regions north of the Alps and in Scandinavia.

Maguire suggests that there was a social significance to this arboreal preoccupation. He writes:

> Whenever a new North European community was founded, the settlers were accustomed to leaving a group of trees, ideally, evergreens, in the center of the main clearing, with one central tree often designated as the mother tree. These trees henceforth functioned as the hub of all social, religious, and political life in the community. They would always be adorned on festive occasions, especially the winter solstice, when everyone in the community desperately needed distraction from the ravages of the severe North European winter.[7]

Among the Celtic peoples evergreen trees and oak trees were decorated with apples and mistletoe to ward off evil spirits at the winter solstice. A particular variety of evergreen oak was associated with the Oak King, a popular godlike figure who was seen as dying for part of the year but as immortal after the winter solstice had begun.

The Norse people linked the solstice tree to Ygg Drasil, an evergreen ash that figured prominently in their creation story. Odin, the father of the gods, spent nine nights hanging from this tree in order to learn the mysteries of existence and to obtain enlightenment.

Later celebrations in honor of Odin included candles, placed in a circle around the solstice tree. Since Odin was considered a light-bearer, a large oak log was burned on December 21. This event was called Yule (from Yolnir, another name for Odin).

The Druids also honored Odin by placing apples on oak and fir tree branches to thank him for their fruitfulness. Small cakes and lighted candles were placed in the boughs of the trees.

One final link between Christianity and earlier religions is the visitation of the Wise Men or Magi, recorded only in St. Matthew's Gospel. These visitors "from the East" are thought to have been Zoroastrian priests, or astrologers, representatives of a religion that emerged in Persia in the sixth century before the Christian Era. Founded by Zoroaster, it is a complicated amalgam of dualism and conflict, characterized by joyfulness, activism and an advanced social ethic. Its holy book is the Avest and its god, Ahura Mazda, the Wise Lord.[8]

Sheryl Ann Karas, in her wonderfully evocative collection of folk tales, argues forcefully that there is a universality of values that centered in the symbolism of trees. From the Cedars of Lebanon to the Mayans to the ancient Lapps in Finland there is a continuity of ancient worship which even the most rigorous Christian apologists could not extirpate. She observes:

> The evergreen played an influential role in the spiritual life
> of early societies throughout the world. Archaeological and

anthropological evidence indicates that veneration of the tree dates from at least 4000 years before Christ. Its pervasive symbolism was central to primitive cosmologies, the beliefs about the universe which laid the foundation for every major religion, including Christianity. These pagan beliefs survive to this day embedded in religious rituals and myths as well as in secular customs, legends and fairy tales.[9]

She also argues, "The connection between the Christmas Tree and the sacred tree is quite clear. . . . The persistence of the tree makes it apparent that its symbolism was more important than the form of its worship.[10]

As Christianity began to subsume the cultural life of the peoples it converted, an inevitable conflict arose between the new religion and exponents of older faiths. The establishment of the Church as the only legally prescribed religion of the Empire in 380 settled the question at the highest, most formal level. It also led to a ruthless persecution of those the Church now labeled "pagans." Centuries of animosity and conflict were the result of Establishment, though its pattern of repression varied from region to region. There were also intense differences of opinion within the Christian community, giving rise to alternative Christian groups, e.g., the Donatists, Marcionites, Nestorians, Monophyites, and many other "heresies."

One thing most Christian leaders tended to agree upon was the necessity of uprooting the old religions. While some Church Fathers like St. Hilary of Poitiers counseled forbearance, tolerance and persuasion, the majority engaged in efforts to reshape the culture in a Christian direction.

Wherever Christianity penetrated, Christmas followed and became enmeshed in local culture. When St. Augustine of Canterbury re-introduced the faith into England, he used Christmas Day as the time for the baptism of ten thousand converts in 598. A French church synod, the Council of Tours, in 567, declared a twelve-day period of worship and celebration from Christmas to Epiphany. The Synod of Mainz established the holiday in

Germany in 813, while in Norway King Haakon the Good made Christmas a holy day in the middle of the tenth century. The laws of Ethelred (991–1016) ordained that Christmas was to be a time of peace and concord, when strife and war making would cease.[11]

At the same time Church authorities tried to uproot the remaining pre-Christian winter festivals, especially the practices associated with the Kalends. At least forty church councils, ranging from Spain, England, Germany, Italy, Antioch, France, Northern Africa, and Constantinople, denounced the Kalends celebrations from the fourth to the eleventh centuries.[12]

There may have been a three-day period of fasting observed by some Christians as a way to challenge the Kalends merriment. One sermon, originally attributed to St. Augustine of Hippo, but probably written by the sixth century Gallic churchman Caesarius of Arles, urged Christians to fast because "he who on the Kalends shows any civility to foolish men who are wantonly sporting, is undoubtedly a partaker of their sin."[13] He also chides those Christians who do participate as "slaves to gluttony, riotous living, drunkenness and impious dancing."[14]

The city of Rome seemed especially prone to merriment and abuse. St. Boniface, the intrepid missionary apostle to the Germanic peoples, complained in a letter to Pope Zacharias in 742 that many of his Bavarian and Frankish converts had refused to give up "heathen practices" because they had seen wanton processions and general merrymaking on a visit to the "sacred city" of Rome. The pope replied that such things were odious to him and should be to all Christians. The following year the Kalends celebrations were forbidden by a Church council.[15]

Boniface, it seems, had a continual struggle with stubborn pagans in his new realm. While successfully converting many of the common people, he failed to convince the rulers of the Alemanic and Frankish tribes that Christianity was superior to their indigenous religions. Upon returning from a visit to Rome, Boniface discovered that the Alemanic leader Gundhar was preparing to sacrifice his oldest son to the god Thor beneath a giant oak tree. Boniface proceeded to chop down the sacred tree, legend says, and a small fir tree appeared behind the oak. Boniface directed that the wood of the fallen oak tree be used in the construction of a monastery. The lowly fir tree thus became a symbol of Christian triumph over paganism and was celebrated in folklore and legend for many centuries.[16]

As the Christian calendar grew in complexity, soon enveloping virtually the entire year with sacred meaning and special events, a distinctive folklore, imagery and iconography of Christmas developed. Poetry, drama, popular devotion and liturgy interacted. Each nation contributed insights and customs of its own. One should not ignore the contribution of folklore to the understanding of popular religion or as a factor in social history. As Sheryl Karas argues, "Although folklore is often neglected in historical studies of cultural phenomena, no other medium can so colorfully and accurately portray the daily life, beliefs and attitudes of a particular society."[17]

It was inevitable, perhaps, that Western Catholic Christendom would have difficulty extricating its rites from popular pre-Christian customs. There was a tension between the church leaders' desires to fully Christianize society by rejecting the non-Christian or natural elements in culture and those who wished to retain the non-Christian practices and endow them with new meanings and symbols.

Clement Miles, writing in 1912, advanced a view held by many scholars:

> The struggle between the ascetic principle of self-mortification, world-renunciation, absorption in a transcendent ideal, and the natural human striving towards earthly joy and well-being, is, perhaps, the most interesting aspect of the history of Christianity; it is certainly shown in an absorbingly interesting way in the development of the Christian feast of the Nativity. The conflict is keen at first; the Church authorities fight tooth and nail against these relics of heathenism, these devilish rites; but mankind's instinctive paganism is insuppressible, the practices

continue as ritual, though losing much of their meaning, and the Church, weary of denouncing, comes to wink at them, while the pagan joy in earthly life begins to colour her own festival.[18]

Pope Gregory I may have inaugurated a new toleration when, in a letter to Abbot Mellitus in 601, he encouraged the Christianization of existing practices among the Anglo Saxon peoples in England. He said:

> Because they are wont to slay many oxen in sacrifices to demons, some solemnity should be put in the place of this, so that on the day of the dedication of the churches, or the nativities of the holy martyrs whose relics are placed there, they may make for themselves tabernacles of branches of trees around those churches which have been changed from heathen temples, and may celebrate the solemnity with religious feasting. Nor let them now sacrifice animals to the Devil, but to the praise of God kill animals for their own eating, and render thanks to the Giver of all for their abundance; so that while some outward joys are retained for them, they may more readily respond to inward joys. For from obdurate minds it is undoubtedly impossible to cut off everything at once, because he who strives to ascend to the highest place rises by degrees or steps and not by leaps.[19]

The Christianization of culture produced several customs associated with Christmas, including legends relating to plants and herbs, which were said to be endowed with certain theological traits or symbolic of events in religious history.

A curious custom originating in the East led indirectly to the modern Christmas tree observances. Francis X. Weiser describes this intriguing story:

> Christmas Eve is the feast day of our first parents, Adam and Eve. They are commemorated as saints in the calendars of the Eastern Churches (Greeks, Syrians, Copts). Under the influence of this oriental practice, their veneration spread also in the West and became very popular toward the end of the first millennium

of the Christian era. The Latin Church has never officially introduced their feast, though it did not prohibit their popular veneration. . . . In Germany the custom began in the sixteenth century of putting up a Paradise tree in the homes. This was a fir tree laden with apples, and from it developed our modern Christmas tree.[20]

The Paradise tree probably originated in the eleventh century revival of religious drama, performed in churches on sacred occasions. These mystery plays presented the Christian story in dramatic form and were popular with everyday people. The Paradise play, telling the tale of Adam and Eve's expulsion from the Garden of Eden, was traditionally presented during Advent. Weiser adds, "Under the influence of medieval religious mystery pictures, the Paradise tree stood not only for the 'Tree of Sin' but also for the 'Tree of Life.' As such, it bore, besides the apples (fruit of sin), wafers representing the Holy Eucharist (fruit of life)."[21]

In the western regions of Germany people began to combine the Paradise tree with the Christmas light custom; thus, the tradition of a lighted tree began. In Alsace there is an early mention of this custom in 1521. By 1605 a manuscript from Strasbourg suggests the widespread popularity of the custom.[22]

More lavish decorations were now acceptable in the sanctuaries. Weiser says, "After the time of the persecutions the Church soon approved and accepted the practice of decorating both the house of God and the Christian home with plants and flowers on the Feast of the Lord's Nativity."[23]

Plants sacred to the Druids, viz. mistletoe, were originally forbidden by the Church's rulers. One exception was the custom of bringing a bundle of mistletoe into the sanctuary of the Cathedral of York. It was explained that the plant, considered to have healing qualities by the Druids, was a symbol of Christ's role as the divine healer of nations.[24]

The holly was more favorably accepted by Christians in northern Europe. It was considered a symbol of Moses's burning bush and the love of God that filled the Virgin Mary's heart.

Its red berries were symbolic of the blood of Christ.[25]

Holly was also endowed with special powers against witchcraft and lightning, which fueled its popularity during the superstitious Middle Ages.[26]

The ivy was associated with the Roman god of wine, Bacchus, and was thus denied Christian acceptance. But romantic poets argued that the delicate little plant symbolized human weakness and therefore it gradually gained approval as a Christmas decoration.[27]

The ancient Roman symbol of triumph and joy, the laurel, was "greatly cherished as a Christmas plant in bygone centuries and was the first plant used as Christmas decoration," says Weiser.[28] In fact Tertullian records that it was used by early Roman Christians as a celebratory adornment in honor of Christ's Nativity.[29]

Finally, the poinsettia, a native of Mexico, is called the "flower of the Holy Night" and is associated with a miraculous Christmas Eve legend.[30] The rosemary is honored because it was said to be the bush used by Mary to dry the garments of Jesus during the Holy Family's exile into Egypt. Rosemary is also invoked as an aid against evil spirits, if it is used as a church decoration on Christmas Day.[31]

Even the lowly herbs "come with many legends and are particularly celebrated during the holidays," writes Nancy Walz.[32] Walz says that mistletoe "will protect your family from demons," that thyme is the herb of bravery, lavender the herb of virtue, and statice and tansy are symbols of everlasting life.[33] The "pennyroyal blooms at midnight when the Christmas bells ring. The white flowers of bedstraw became gold with the Christ Child's radiance," and the Christmas rose opened at the hour of Jesus's birth. Rosemary, originally white, turned blue when the Virgin Mary placed her blue cloak over its flowers.[34]

Notes

1. Jack Maguire, *O Christmas Tree!* (New York: Avon, 1992), p. 5.
2. *The Works of Lucian of Samosata* (Oxford: Oxford University Press, 1905, vol. 4), p. 114.
3. Clement A. Miles, *Christmas in Ritual and Tradition, Christian and Pagan* (London: T. Fisher Unwin, 1912), pp. 168–69.
4. Maguire, p. 7.
5. Geoffrey Parrinder, *World Religions* (New York: Facts on File, 1971), p. 187.
6. Miles, p. 23.
7. Maguire, p. 8.
8. Parrinder, pp. 177–81.
9. Sheryl Ann Karas, *The Solstice Evergreen: The History, Folklore and Origins of the Christmas Tree* (Boulder Creek, Calif.: Aslan, 1991), p. 4.
10. Ibid., p. 24.
11. Miles, p. 21.
12. Ibid., p. 169.
13. Ibid., p. 170.
14. Ibid.
15. Ibid., p. 171.
16. Ibid.
17. Karas, p. 1.
18. Miles, p. 26.
19. Ibid., p. 179.
20. Francis X. Weiser, *Handbook of Christian Feasts and Customs* (New York: Harcourt, Brace, 1958), p. 59.
21. Ibid., p. 99.
22. Ibid., pp. 100–101.
23. Ibid., p. 103.
24. W. F. Dawson, *Christmas: Its Origins and Associations* (London: Elliot Stock, 1902), p. 240.
25. T. G. Crippen, *Christmas and Christmas Lore* (London: Blackie, 1923), p. 15.
26. Weiser, p. 105.
27. Crippen, p. 14.
28. Weiser, p. 106.

29. Ibid.

30. Ibid., p. 107.

31. Ibid., p. 106.

32. Nancy Walz, "Of Myths and Mistletoe," *Frederick Magazine* 8 (December 1992), pp. 50–53.

33. Ibid.

34. Ibid. See also Linda Ours Rago, *Herbal Almanac* (Washington, D.C.: Starwood Publications, 1992).

3

Reformers, Puritans,
and Victorians

A certain degeneration of the religious culture of medieval Europe was accompanied by a growth of superstitious practices and a decline in the spiritual underpinnings of holy days. While Clement Miles hailed "the transformation of the Church's Christmas from something austere and metaphysical into something joyous and human, warm and kindly," he also admitted, "the survival of much that is purely pagan, continuing alongside of the celebration of the Nativity, and often little touched by its influence."[1]

Christmas Eve, in particular, was suffused by "a large admixture of paganism,"[2] including the beliefs that animals can speak, that water turns into wine, that the dead revisit their old homes, and that various trolls and auguries can be observed.[3] Crippen contributes this delightful tidbit: "There is an Irish superstition that the gates of Paradise are always open on Christmas Eve; so that anyone dying at that moment enters at once, without going to Purgatory. Grim stories are told of persons who were obviously dying, and were kindly helped out of this world just at the critical moment."[4]

Some Roman Catholic authorities opted for a solely spiritual

Christmas festivity. They resembled some of the Protestant Reformers in their objections. A number of Catholic Church leaders sought to minimize the secular customs which were widely popular. The Reverend Johann Konrad Dannhauer, a canon at Strassbourg Cathedral in Alsace, criticized the decoration of a fir tree as "a trifle with which the people often occupy the Christmas time more than with God's word. . . . Where the habit comes from, I know not. It is a bit of child's play. Far better were it for the children to be dedicated to the spiritual cedar tree, Jesus Christ."[5]

The theologians and apologists for the Protestant Reformation developed and promoted a new *Sola Scriptura* principle, in which the canonical Scriptures agreed upon at the end of the fourth and beginning of the fifth centuries became the sole source of authority for all of Christian life and practice. In doing so, they enshrined as normative a particularly brief period of history, the years 40 to 90 A.D. when the New Testament documents were written. Since only fragmentary and inchoate descriptions of Christian worship and customs appear here, the Reformers rejected almost all subsequent additions and developments. Rejecting the continuous interplay between Scripture and Tradition that animated Catholicism and Eastern Orthodoxy, the Reformers eschewed the celebration of Christmas and other holy days in their quest for the pristine purity of the primitive church.

During the Reformation era, the Lutherans preserved the celebration of Christmas as a major holy day. So did the Church of England, which retained Christmas as a red-letter day and enjoined its communicants to attend divine services and receive the Sacrament of Holy Communion on Christmas, Easter and Pentecost. The English Church also preserved a full-scale liturgy for Christmas, including appointed lessons, collects, and a preface for the ordinary of the Mass. Says J. A. R. Pimlott, the preeminent chronicler of the English Christmas: "Secular celebrations appealed to the love of pleasure, pageantry and colour which was shared by all ranks in the age of Henry VIII, Elizabeth I, Shakespeare and Ben Jonson."[6] And, while "writers and poets paid little attention to the religious aspects of the festival, they showed, unless they were Puritans, a zestful appreciation of the traditional merriment and an apparently sincere belief in the traditional virtues."[7]

The Regal Court, the universities, and the Inns of Court remained steadfast in their observance of Christmas. The English Civil War changed all that.

The victory of Oliver Cromwell and his Puritan Roundheads subjected England to a military dictatorship based on a kind of fundamentalist Protestantism. Everyday life resembled Spain during the Inquisition or Iran today under the reign of the mullahs.

Pimlott places the Puritan opposition to Christmas in this context:

> The Puritan attack upon Christmas was only a minor expression of religious and social ideas which were revolutionary in their impact on the national life in general. Christmas was criticised because of its "Popish" antecedents and because as the chief national holiday it was especially associated with drinking, dancing, play acting, gambling and other evils. The apparently disproportionate attention which it received in the propaganda and counter-propaganda of the Puritans and their opponents showed how much it meant in the lives of English people. The more extreme Puritans attacked it as a manifestation of Rome and the Devil. Royalists and Anglicans exploited it as a symbol of traditional virtues and pleasant old customs which their enemies were determined to destroy.[8]

Ironically, it was the Scottish Presbyterians, whose hatred for Christmas had led to its suppression in 1583, who imposed a ban in England. Scotland had its own version of a Christmas war. In 1618 King James I forced the Scots to accept Christmas and certain other festivals. Twenty years later the increasingly powerful and querulous General Assembly of the semi-established Church of Scotland set this accommodation aside. After 1638 Christmas was again illegal in the land of John Knox.

In 1644 Cromwell's Long Parliament had been reluctant to impose a Christmas ban on England and Wales. But Christmas Day fell on a Wednesday, and the last Wednesday in each month was by law a day of solemn fast and penance. The Scots demanded that the fast day supersede Christmas. The decision was "widely disregarded" according to Pimlott, who observed that the ban "was only effective in the areas which were under Parliamentary control. In the following year the religious but not the secular celebrations were outlawed as a result of another general measure: the substitution of the Presbyterian Directory of Public Prayer for the Book of Common Prayer."[9] This curious action led one wag to observe, "O blessed Reformation! The church doors all shut, and the tavern doors all open!"[10] In 1647 Christmas Day could no longer lawfully be celebrated as a religious or secular holiday. Pimlott describes the reaction, "When Christmas came, there was both passive and active resistance. Some London shops closed in defiance of Parliament and some that stayed open had their windows broken. Officers had to be sent to remove the evergreens from a number of London churches, including St. Margaret's in the shadow of Parliament itself."[11] At first, "Aggressive disobedience was uncommon but noncompliance prevalent," Pimlott concluded.[12]

Succeeding Christmases were wracked by dissension and even violence on the part of those who insisted on their right to celebrate the holiday as their ancestors had done. Pimlott continues, "Lives were lost in riots at Ipswich, skulls were broken at Oxford, and ten thousand men of Kent and Canterbury passed an ominous resolution, saying, 'If they could not have their Christmas Day, they would have the King back on his throne.' "[13] Mobs attacked shopkeepers who opened their doors on Christmas. The Mayor of Canterbury was attacked after he openly proclaimed that "Christmas Day and all other superstitious festivals should be put down."[14]

Parliament was now clearly worried. Support for the restoration of Christmas had taken on political overtones. Moderate Puritans favored allowing dancing and theatrical performances, even though they still wanted a ban on public worship. Moderate Anglicans did not object to the ban on secular entertainments but wished to worship openly. Fanatical Puritans like Hezekiah Woodward wanted total enforcement of the ban. Woodward issued an inflammatory pamphlet in 1656 in which he called Christmas "The old heathen's feasting day, in honour to Saturn their idol-god, the papist's massing day, the profane man's ranting day, the superstitious man's idol day."[15] He also complained of "heathenish customs, popish superstitions, ranting fashions, fearful provocations, horrible abominations committed against the Lord and His Christ on that day and the days following."[16]

Puritan propagandists were certainly not reticent in formulating their rhetoric! William Prynne said that "all pious Christians should eternally abominate Christmas disorders."[17]

Parliament refused to modify its ban. The extremist wing of the ruling party had prevailed. Meeting on Christmas Eve in 1652, the Parliamentarians accepted "a terrible Remonstrance against Christmas day, grounded upon divine Scriptures. Christmas is called "Anti-Christ's masse, and those who observe it as Massemongers and Papists."[18]

A newspaper of that day, The Flying Eagle, reported that "Parliament spent some time in consultation about the abolition of Christmas day, passed orders to that effect, and resolved to sit on the following day, which was commonly called Christmas day."[19]

Parliament ruled that "the 25th of December should not be solemnised in churches or observed in any other way, that town criers should each year remind the people that Christmas Day and other superstitious festivals should not be kept and the markets and shops should stay open."[20]

Practicing members of the Church of England, who were probably the majority of the population, were placed in a fearful dilemma. Any worship conducted according to their rites was prohibited, though enforcement seemed to vary from region to region. The Anglicans were driven into the catacombs, as it were. Pimlott says, "There was comparatively little interference with private worship, and some congregations were allowed to meet under sequestered ministers."[21]

But Puritan authorities seemed to delight in hunting down Christmas worshippers. "Public services at Christmas could not be held without serious risk."[22]

English diarist John Evelyn has left a remarkable account of his indomitable attempts to attend Christmas Communion during the 1650s.

His diary for Christmas Day in 1652 is blunt: "No sermon anywhere, no church being permitted to open, so observed it at home." In 1654 it was the same. "No public offices in churches, but penalties on observers, so I was construed to celebrate it at home." In 1655 sorrow and nostalgia intruded into his diary. "There was no more notice taken of Christmas-day in churches. Cromwell's proclamation was to take place, that none of the Church of England should dare either to preach, or administer Sacraments or teach schools on pain of imprisonment or exile. So this was the mournfulst day that my life had seen . . . The Lord Jesus pity our distressed Church and bring back the captivity of Zion!"[23] Evelyn and his wife and family risked arrest to receive Communion on that sorrowful day.

Two years later, in 1657, Evelyn records another attempt at public worship. It is a chilling account of life in a religious autocracy:

> 25th Dec., 1657 I went to London with my wife, to celebrate Christmas-day, Mr Gunning preaching in Exeter chapel, on Micah vii, 2. Sermon ended, as he was giving us the Holy Sacrament, the chapel was surrounded with soldiers, and all the communicants and assembly surprised and kept prisoners by them, some in the house, others carried away. It fell to my share to be confined to a room in the house, where yet I was permitted to dine with the master of it, the Countess of Dorset, Lady Hatton, and some others of quality who invited me. In the afternoon came Colonel Whalley, Goffe, and others, from Whitehall to examine us one by one; some they committed to

the Marshal, some to prison. When I came before them, they took my name and abode, examined me why, contrary to the ordinance made, that none should any longer observe the superstitious time of the Nativity (so esteemed by them), I durst offend, and particularly be at Common Prayers, which they told me was but the mass in English, and particularly pray for Charles Stuart; for which we had no scripture. I told them we did not pray for Charles Stuart, but for all Christian Kings, Princes, and Governors. They replied, in so doing we prayed for the King of Spain, too, who was their enemy and a Papist, with other frivolous and ensnaring questions, and much threatening; and, finding no colour to detain me, they dismissed me with much pity of my ignorance. These were men of high flight and above ordinances, and spake spiteful things of our Lord's Nativity. As we went up to receive the Sacrament, the miscreants held their muskets against us, as if they would have shot us at the altar, but yet suffering us to finish the office of Communion, as perhaps not having instructions what to do, in case they found us in that action. So I got home late the next day, blessed be God![24]

In 1658 there was no public service, says Evelyn, but some observed the Nativity in private.

Religious authoritarians have always delighted in repressing dissenters and in rooting out heretics. The Cromwell era gave the English people a taste of religious tyranny. As in all autocracies, Commonwealth England abounded in absurd legislation. Parliament and local magistrates banned Christmas dinners and plum puddings, and one magistrate fined Lord Fairfax five shillings in 1655 for attending a comedy at Christmas.[25]

Always on the lookout for miscreants, one Puritan divine, Sir John Birkenhead, issued a pamphlet in 1652 accusing an independent preacher, Hugh Peters, of preaching against Christmas but consuming two mince pies for his dinner. An Anglican bishop thought the irony delicious and wrote, "Though the religious part of this holy time is laid aside, yet the eating part is observed by the holiest of the brethren."[26]

Militant Puritans even complained that their parliamentarians were insufficiently faithful. One member charged that too many of his fellow legislators were absent from a 1656 Christmas day debate. He feared that some backsliders were quietly observing Christmas in the privacy of their homes.[27] Another speaker in the House of Commons said his fellow citizens were "poor simple creatures who love superstitious festivals and unholy holydays."[28] A Puritan preacher, Calamy, lamented in a sermon to the House of Lords at Westminster Abbey, "I have known some that have preferred Christmas Day before the Lord's Day."[29]

Parliament insisted on conducting business as usual every Christmas Day from 1644 to 1656 but many shopkeepers continued to close for the day. "Evergreen decorations were put up throughout the City of London, and the Lord Mayor and City Marshall had to ride about setting fire to them," observed Miles.[30]

For some still unknown reason, the Puritans held a special wrath for mince-pie and plum pudding. An anonymous doggerel claimed that "plum broth was Popish and mincepie oh that was sheer idolatry." Fletcher's "Christmas Day," a 1656 poem, called the mince pie "idolatry in crust! Babylon's whore."[31]

A veritable "Paper war" between Christmas-lovers and Christmas-haters enlivened the seventeenth century English publishing world. As early as 1633 William Prynne, a Puritan lawyer, published "Histrio Mastrix," a condemnation of Christmas. He was committed to the Tower of London, prosecuted in the Star Chamber, fined £5,000 (to the King no less!), expelled from the University of Oxford and the legal profession. He was forced to stand in the pillory, and his book was burned.[32] Such was King Charles I's fondness for the holiday. Charles also caused to be published the "Seventeen Sermons on the Nativity" preached by Bishop Lancelot Andrewes before King James I at Whitehall. This unique theological work, which revealed the importance of Christmas to both the Anglican Church and the Monarchy, remained in print three centuries later.[33]

Another anti-Christmas pamphlet was called "The Arraignment, Conviction and Imprisonment of Christmas," which includes these choice words: "All Popish, prelatical, Jesuitical, ignorant, Judaical and superstitious persons ask after the very old grey-bearded gentleman called Christmas. Whoever finds him again shall be rewarded with a benediction from the Pope and forty kisses from wanton wenches."[34] In "The Vindication of Father Christmas," published in 1653, Christmas laments the treatment he had received from the Puritans but promises, "Welcome or not, I am come."[35]

The restoration of the monarchy under the merry monarch, Charles II, brought an official return of Christmas. By all accounts, this was one of the most widely popular decisions among the masses of everyday dwellers of Albion.

Still, even the return of Christmas to national life did not restore its centrality. Miles says, "With the Restoration Christmas naturally came back to full recognition, though it may be doubted whether it has ever been quite the same thing since the Puritan Revolution."[36]

In the seventeenth and eighteenth centuries, Pimlott says, "To an increasing extent Christmas was indifferently observed even by church-goers, and many people entirely neglected their religious duties."[37] Just before Charles Dickens made emotional appeals for renewed charity to the less fortunate, Christmas, says Pimlott, "lost in spiritual content and emotional appeal."[38]

Especially among dissenters, the English term for evangelical Protestants, did hostility remain strong throughout the eighteenth and nineteenth centuries. Pimlott observes, "As the direct heirs of the Puritans, the Dissenters were positively hostile to any form of observance, and especially among the middle classes they exerted an influence disproportionate to their numbers. Their opposition was often pedantic, and they still believed that it was heathenish and popish to keep up such minor customs as evergreens, the yule log and mumming."[39]

Government departments and industries, however, still allowed workers a day off on Christmas, much to the dismay of the Ebeneezer Scrooges of the business world.

By the mid and late Victorian Era, new developments had

conspired to change the nature of Christmas. "It developed into a preeminently family festival, centered mainly on the children," observes Pimlott, and "the customs inherited from the past were reshaped to meet rapidly changing social and economic conditions."[40] He also adds that "the forces which recast the traditional celebrations were derived mainly from the religious revival and the humanitarian and romantic movements."[41]

The religious revival to which he alluded was the Methodist movement, which in England favored Christmas worship services, in contrast to many of its early American brethren. Also, the Anglo-Catholic Oxford Movement emphasized restoration of antiquarian and European religious practices and customs.

Even some Protestant Dissenters, now called Nonconformists, began to relent and hold services on Christmas, because many of their members were defecting to the Anglican Church.[42]

The Bank Holiday Act of 1871 made Boxing Day, the day after Christmas, a holiday, and the Holiday Extension Act of 1875 applied this to commerce and industry. The *London Times* was hostile, calling Boxing Day "the Saturnalia of our people, secured to it now by Act of Parliament."[43]

There were still holdouts among certain religious groups, described by essayist Charles Lamb in 1827 as "Puritans, Muggletonians, Anabaptists, Quakers and that Unwassailing Crew."[44]

Edmund Gosse, who belonged to the Plymouth Brethren in his youth, describes his childhood encounter with Christmas in his memoir *Father and Son:*

> On the subject of all feasts of the Church he held views of an almost grotesque peculiarity. He looked upon each of them as nugatory and worthless, but the keeping of Christmas appeared to him by far the most hateful, and nothing less than an act of idolatry. "The very word is Popish," he used to exclaim, "Christ's Mass!" pursing his lips with the gesture of one who tastes assafoetida by accident. Then he would adduce the antiquity of the so-called feast, adapted from horrible heathen rites, and itself a soiled relic of the abominable Yule-tide. He

would denounce the horrors of Christmas until it almost made me blush to look at a holly-berry.

On Christmas Day of this year 1857 our villa saw a very unusual sight. My father had given strictest charge that no difference whatever was to be made in our meals on that day; the dinner was to be neither more copious than usual nor less so. He was obeyed, but the servants, secretly rebellious, made a small plum pudding for themselves. Early in the afternoon, the maids kindly remarked that the poor dear child ought to have a bit anyhow, and wheedled me into the kitchen, where I ate a slice of plum-pudding. Shortly I began to feel a pain inside which in my frail state was inevitable, and my conscience smote me violently. At length I could bear my spiritual anguish no longer, and bursting into the study I called out: "Oh Papa, Papa, I have eaten the flesh offered to idols!" It took some time between my sobs to explain what had happened. Then my father sternly said: "Where is the accursed thing?" I explained that as much as was left of it was still on the kitchen table. He took me by the hand, and ran with me into the midst of the startled servants, seized what remained of the pudding, and with the plate in one hand and me still tight in the other, ran till we reached the dust-heap, when he flung the idolatrous confectionery onto the middle of the ashes, and then raked it down into the mass. The suddenness, the violence, the velocity of this extraordinary act made an impression on my memory which nothing will ever efface.[45]

Only in Presbyterian Scotland was Christmas still largely ignored until after World War II, except among Episcopalians and Roman Catholics. Even some Presbyterians seemed to enjoy the holiday, however, leading the *Scotsman* to comment acidly in 1905 that "The Presbyterians have adopted the Yule of the heathen without sacrifice of principles."[46]

Even the Scots held a tenacious preference for many pre-Christian customs. They merely transferred them from Christmas to New Year's Day, the period called "the Daft Days" in Scots folklore and culture. In the Gaelic-speaking districts of the Highlands, customs of pre-Reformation and pre-Christian antiquity survived into the early twentieth century.[47]

Great Britain and the United States shared so many cross-cultural experiences that their Christmas celebrations developed in almost parallel ways.

A similar evolution in the religious communities of both Britain and America has been noted. The conservative Protestant "Free Churches" have adapted the Christmas festival with the proverbial enthusiasm of the convert, and even the Church of Scotland did not oppose the declaration of Christmas as a legal holiday. The *London Times* in 1954 reported with amazement "the abandon with which Presbyterian Scotland celebrates the Christmas festival, now restored in popular favor after 400 years of virtual banishment."[48]

Meanwhile, Nativity plays flourished in the Church of England, some being written by writers of the stature of John Masefield and Dorothy Sayers. Creches and Christmas trees appear routinely in churches, railway stations, and public libraries.[49] "Powerful vested interests and the forces of conservatism are particularly strong where the observance of Christmas is concerned,"[50] observed Pimlott, leading him to conclude, "There has probably never been a time since Cromwell when Christmas has been more universally acceptable."[51]

Notes

1. Clement A. Miles, *Christmas in Ritual and Tradition, Christian and Pagan* (London: T. Fisher Unwin, 1912), p. 27.
2. Ibid., p. 233.
3. Ibid., pp. 233–37.
4. T. G. Crippen, *Christmas and Christmas Lore* (London: Blackie, 1923), p. 169.
5. Quoted in Earl W. Count, *4000 Years of Christmas* (New York: Henry Schuman, 1948), p. 75.
6. J. A. R. Pimlott, *The Englishman's Christmas: A Social History*

(Atlantic Highlands, N.J.: Humanities Press Inc., 1978), p. 30.

7. Ibid.

8. Ibid., p. 49.

9. Ibid., pp. 51–52.

10. Quoted in Pimlott, p. 52.

11. Pimlott, p. 52.

12. Ibid., p. 53.

13. Ibid., p. 52.

14. "Canterbury Christmas: A True Relation of the Insurrection at Canterbury (1647)," reprinted in William Kean Seymour and John Smith, *Happy Christmas* (Philadelphia: Westminster, 1968), pp. 172–73.

15. Pimlott, p. 53.

16. Ibid., pp. 53–54.

17. Quoted in Seymour and Smith, p. 172.

18. Ibid., p. 174.

19. Ibid.

20. Pimlott, p. 54.

21. Ibid.

22. Ibid., p. 55.

23. Seymour and Smith, p. 174.

24. Ibid., p. 175.

25. Pimlott, p. 58.

26. Ibid.

27. Ibid., p. 57.

28. Miles, p. 185.

29. Ibid.

30. Ibid.

31. Pimlott, p. 46.

32. W. F. Dawson, *Christmas: Its Origins and Associations* (London: Elliot Stock, 1902), pp. 199–200.

33. Ibid., pp. 193–95.

34. Ibid., p. 209.

35. Ibid., p. 212.

36. Miles, p. 185.

37. Pimlott, p. 60.

38. Ibid., p. 83.

39. Ibid., p. 61.

40. Ibid., p. 85.

41. Ibid., p. 86.
42. Ibid., p. 92.
43. Quoted in Pimlott, p. 95.
44. Pimlott, p. 90.
45. Quoted in Pimlott, pp. 91–92.
46. Quoted in Pimlott, p. 93.
47. Crippen, pp. 181–82.
48. Quoted in Pimlott, p. 149.
49. Pimlott, pp. 151–52.
50. Ibid., p. 177.
51. Ibid., p. 179.

4

Christmas in America:
From Prohibition to Legalization
to Acceptance

Puritan Massachusetts, a theocracy, forbade even the private re-
membrance of Christmas, forbade employers to excuse their employees from work, and imposed fines on those who chose to
observe the birthday of Jesus. The Massachusetts law of 1659
was severe. It read: "Anybody who is found observing, by ab-
stinence from labor, feasting or any other way any such days
as Christmas day, shall pay for every such offense five shillings."[1]

As early as 1621 Governor Bradford of the Plymouth Colony
publicly reprimanded several young men who maintained that
working on Christmas violated their conscience! Connecticut's
early laws also forbade its citizens to "read the Common Prayer,
keep Christmas or saints days."

The eminent Christmas historian Phillip Snyder describes
what happened after Christmas was restored in England and
in New England:

> When Christmas came out of hiding in England following the
> restoration of Charles II in 1660, the Puritans in New England

55

boldly resisted the efforts of the Crown to establish the Anglican Church there. In the Massachusetts Bay Colony, Anglicans were so unwelcome that they were denied citizenship. In 1665 an Episcopal chaplain arrived in Boston, but there was no church in which he could hold services. In 1686, when Sir Edmund Andros was sent over to unite New York and New Jersey with the New England colonies, it was one of the complaints against him that under his administration, Anglican Church services were held in Old South Church in Boston on Sunday afternoons by force of arms. Governor Andros went to the Episcopal service on Christmas Day that year guarded by a redcoat on his right and a captain on his left. In 1689 Boston revolted and put Andros in prison. In 1706 a Puritan mob broke windows in the King's Chapel in Boston because Anglican worshippers were holding a Christmas service there. . . . The Puritans made all of New England (with the exception of freethinking Rhode Island) a stronghold for anti-Christmas Reformation doctrine. Although the mid-Atlantic colonies acquired ethnically diverse populations holding varying beliefs—more than twenty different religious denominations were represented—by far the most numerous sect was the Christmas-disdaining Scotch-Irish Presbyterians. So altogether there was precious little Christmas spirit from Massachusetts (which then included Maine) to Pennsylvania in pre-Revolutionary days.[2]

While the law forbidding the celebration of Christmas was repealed in Massachusetts in 1681, local custom frowned on it. One Puritan official, a judge named Sewell, observed in 1685: "Some, somehow observe the day, but are vexed, I believe, that the Body of the People Profane it; and, blessed be God, no Authority yet to compel them to keep it."[3] Businesses remained open on Christmas, as did public schools, until the late 1880s.

Another New Englander, Henry Ward Beecher, a Congregationalist pastor and probably the most prominent clergyperson in nineteenth-century America, described the disdain for Christmas that was widespread during his childhood. Writing in 1874, he remembered:

To me Christmas is a foreign day, and I shall die so. When I was a boy I wondered what Christmas was. I knew there was such a time, because we had an Episcopal church in our town and I saw them dressing it with evergreens. . . . A little later I understood it was a Romish institution, kept up by the Romish Church. Brought up in the strictest state of New England, brought up in the most literal style of worship . . . I passed all my youth without any knowledge of Christmas, and so I have no associations with the day.[4]

In Virginia and the Carolinas, where the Church of England was established, Christmas was observed with appropriate if low-keyed celebration. The Anglicans had always revered Christmas, considering it one of the three great festivals (along with Easter and Pentecost) of the Church Year. Home and family celebrations rivaled those of the Church. Maryland, founded as a refuge for Catholics, allowed and encouraged Christmas observances. Lutherans and Moravians in Pennsylvania and the Dutch Reformed Christians in New York also celebrated Christmas. As a general rule the Congregationalists, Quakers, Presbyterians, Methodists and Baptists shunned the holiday.

It should be noted that the former French and Spanish colonies in the South observed Christmas. Daniel J. Foley observed:

Florida can lay claim to the earliest observance of Christmas in America, citing the visit of DeSoto in 1539. Then there is the account of a Christmas observance at St. Augustine in 1565. John Bartram, noted Philadelphia botanist, described his Christmas among the Indians near Mobile in 1777. The French who settled Missouri in the 1730s firmly established the observance of both Christmas and New Year's Day.[5]

These religious differences can be seen in a *New York Times* report of December 26, 1855. Its correspondent noted, "The churches of the Presbyterians, Baptists and Methodists were not open. They do not accept the day as a holy one, but the Episcopal, Catholic and German churches were all open and decked with evergreens."

Religious, cultural and even class differences dominated attitudes toward Christmas all during the nineteenth century. Around 1800 the daughter of Connecticut's governor, Jonathan Trumbull, looked far and wide for any church in New York City that observed the day with religious services. Other than Roman Catholics, only the Episcopalians did so. "We went to church (Anglican) in the morning, and it was all decorated with evergreen bushes," wrote Harriet Trumbull.[6] In December 1810 the *Philadelphia Democratic Press* commented, "The greater part of the citizens of Pennsylvania pay no regard to such days as Christmas."[7]

A half century later the antagonisms were still there. The Reverend Henry Harbaugh, a Reformed Church pastor, had been exiled to an isolated and predominantly Scotch-Irish community near Harrisburg, Pennsylvania, for the crime of promoting Christmas too avidly among his fellow evangelicals. He held the local Presbyterians in contempt for their indifference to his favorite holiday. He wrote in 1867, "Here where I am living in the western Pennsylvania hills, they want to hear nothing of Christmas. They spend the day working as on any other day. Their children grow up knowing nothing of brightly lit Christmas trees, nor Christmas presents. God have mercy on these Presbyterians, these pagans."[8]

As late as 1886 the widely read Methodist newspaper, *The Christian Advocate,* described Christmas as a day "on which more sin and sacrilege and pagan foolishness is committed than on any other day of the year."[9] The American Methodists of that era also vigorously opposed attendance at the theater, cardplaying, dancing, mixed bathing at the seashore, and other activities deemed frivolous and sinful.

Even in colonies which were permissive, there was little or no acknowledgment of the holiday by local magistrates. It was not a legal holiday. Businesses and schools did not as a general rule cease their activities. Even the White House and Congress conducted business if necessary. The major presidential "event" in those days was the New Year's Day "levee," when ordinary citizens lined up to greet their Chief Executive.

In the nineteenth century religious, folkloric, ethnic, and regional factors converged to make Christmas a distinctive holiday. The increasing popularity of Yuletide was demonstrated by the legal recognition of Christmas.

Alabama was the first state to acknowledge the special character of Christmas Day when it formally declared it a legal holiday in 1836. Twenty-eight states followed suit within three decades, thirteen of them doing so during the Civil War. Most states also accorded legal recognition at the same time to Thanksgiving Day, the Fourth of July and New Year's Day.

James Barnett observes:

> It is significant that initial legal recognition of December 25th originated in relation to economic and commercial interests. Thus, Christmas Day was first recognized as an occasion when promissory notes could not be collected on the day immediately preceding or following the holiday. In some instances judicial activities on Christmas Day were forbidden by law. Provisions for school holidays, closing of banks and offices of state governments were enacted later in the century.[10]

Barnett also suggests that Christmas was becoming a uniquely "American" occasion which transcended regional and cultural differences. He writes:

> One suspects that the legal recognition accorded December 25th was a sign of an emerging national self-consciousness which found symbolic expression in the Christmas festival. This idea receives slight confirmation from the fact that a large number of states recognized this day during the Civil War years when the sense of national identity attained a new intensity. Furthermore, the fact that in 1870 Congress established December 25th as a special day for the District of Columbia indicates that the celebration had attained considerable national popularity by that time.[11]

By 1890 all of the states and territories had legally recognized Christmas. This would appear to have made Christmas an official legal holiday in the United States, but the actual situation is more complicated. As Alvin Rosenbaum explains, "Unlike virtually every other country in the world, the United States does not celebrate national holidays. Instead, each state adopts its own observances, along with federal holidays, decreed for employees of the federal government."[12]

Christmas Day became a paid holiday for federal employees in 1885. Interestingly, the U.S. Congress was officially in session on Christmas Day from 1789 to 1856, with the exceptions of 1800, 1817, and 1828. Congress also met on Christmas during the Civil War years of 1861 and 1862.[13]

Christmas also seemed to have served as a kind of ecumenical bridge among Christians who still bitterly disagreed over doctrines, theology, lifestyle, and church-state questions. In her study, *How Christmas Came to the Sunday Schools,* Katherine Lambert Richards traced the gradual acceptance of the religious celebration of Christmas among the formerly opposed Protestant churches. She found an almost complete *volte-face* by the end of the century. She discovered that "within the Protestant churches Christmas had emerged from its Roman Catholic associations and had been recognized as a part of the general inheritance of Christendom."[14]

Other historians confirm this trend. Philip Snyder says, "Once launched, the Protestant church Christmas was carried forward by an irresistible momentum. By the last decade of the nineteenth century, all the major Protestant denominations had adopted Christmas observances with the proverbial enthusiasm of the convert."[15]

James Barnett suggests that the "general observance of Christmas by different churches had a unifying social effect on their members" and the "participation in common-folk aspects of the celebration probably promoted tolerance of denominational differences."[16]

Ruth Cole Kainen writes, "Sometime during the second half

of the nineteenth century, the holiday-hating Scotch-Irish made accommodation with Christmas, perhaps because the possibility of extracting good behavior from rebellious youngsters outweighed other disadvantages of Christmas."[17] People made their own peace with Christmas, according to preferences or upbringing. Robert Blair Risk wrote in 1912 that his Presbyterian parents never allowed a Christmas tree but did permit Santa Claus.[18]

The Christmas-affirming religious and ethnic communities continued their celebrations with religious conviction and culinary conviviality. Regions like the Pennsylvania Dutch Country were noted for the richness of their holiday activities.

The multiculturalism of the United States contributed to the popularity of Christmas. Americans of Dutch and Belgian descent celebrated St. Nicholas Day on December 6, while Swedish-Americans revered December 13, the Feast of St. Lucia. Filipino-Americans begin their Christmas festivities on December 16, when they erect nativity scenes called *Belens*.

Many Hispanic-Americans begin the Christmas season with the feast of Our Lady of Guadaloupe on December 12. Kainen notes that "The Spanish celebrated Christmas in New Mexico long before the Puritans landed at Plymouth."[19]

The celebration of Christmas in Hawaii reveals how an admixture of cultures and religions reshaped the holiday in the last state to enter the Union, and the only one where Asian-Americans comprise a majority of the population.

While the first Christmas celebration can be traced to a British ship lying in the harbor at Waimea Bay in 1786, the first island-wide observance came in 1856 when King Kamehameha IV issued a royal proclamation making Christmas and Thanksgiving a joint feast on December 25, 1856. Six years later he proclaimed Christmas a national holiday and put the authority of the monarchy behind it. Kainen describes this remarkably gala occasion:

> The King sent to the mountains for cypress, and offered myrtle, orange bows, and flowers from his own gardens for decorating the Episcopal Cathedral. The Fort Street Calvinist Church gave

in to the irresistible force. In front of the building, a huge Christmas tree was decorated with some 200 small lights and hung with gifts for over 70 students. . . . On Christmas Eve all were ready. From the top of its dome to the street below, the Roman Catholic Cathedral blazed with lights. When the midnight service began in the Anglican Church, the altar was lit with the King's own candelabra. When the service ended around 1 a.m., guns were fired from a battery on a peak nearby, and flaming tar barrels were sent rolling down from the crest. Then the King and the bishop led a slow procession from the church to the palace, followed by a choir of twenty islanders singing Christmas hymns and bearing native Kukui-nut torches. From time to time the assembly stopped along the way to light innumerable green candles.[20]

The festivity was then topped off with fireworks, champagne punch, the singing of "Good King Wenceslas" and the National Anthem.[21]

Christmas was always popular with the island's large Filipino and Portuguese Catholic population, and it has become acceptable to Buddhists as well. Kainen adds:

Oriental and Christian holidays fuse into one long period of festivity, which begins with *Bodhi*, an important Buddhist holiday when Japanese dances and cultural programs are featured, and ends with Chinese New Year. For Christmas, some popular Christmas carols have been refitted with words from Buddhist *sutras*, Oriental sacred writing. . . . Along the streets and highways, palm trees strung with colored lights are a common sight. Even the sacred Indian Banyan tree is so arrayed.[22]

Creches in Hawaii are likely to feature orchids, pineapples and mynah birds.

Notes

1. James H. Barnett, *The American Christmas: A Study in National Culture* (New York: Macmillan, 1954), p. 3.

2. Phillip Snyder, *December 25th* (New York: Dodd, Mead & Co., 1986), pp. xvi, xvii.

3. Quoted in G. W. Curtis, "Christmas," *Harpers New Monthly Magazine,* 68 (December 1883), p. 13.

4. Quoted in Robert Meyers, *Celebrations: The Complete Book of American Holidays* (New York: Doubleday, 1972), pp. 315–16.

5. Daniel J. Foley, *The Christmas Tree* (Philadelphia: Chilton Co., 1960), p. 69.

6. Quoted in Snyder, *December 25th,* p. xix.

7. Ibid., p. xviii.

8. Ibid.

9. Ibid., p. xiv.

10. Barnett, p. 19.

11. Ibid., p. 21.

12. Alvin Rosenbaum, *A White House Christmas* (Washington, D.C.: The Preservation Press, 1992), p. 87.

13. Ibid., p. 88.

14. Katherine Lambert Richards, *How Christmas Came to the Sunday Schools* (New York: Dodd, Mead & Co., 1934), p. 157.

15. Snyder, p. 277.

16. Barnett, p. 22.

17. Ruth Cole Kainen, *America's Christmas Heritage* (New York: Funk & Wagnalls, 1969), pp. 85–86.

18. Ibid., p. 86.

19. Ibid., p. 143.

20. Ibid., pp. 229–30.

21. Ibid., p. 230.

22. Ibid., p. 231.

5

Presidential and Other Promoters

As odd as it may seem, the primary promoters of a public proclamation of Christmas have been the presidents of the United States
since the early part of this century. Before the 1920s, few presidents paid much public notice to the holiday. Their observances,
if any, were related to their own religious proclivities, and per-
sonality preferences. George Washington, for example, enjoyed
the familial warmth of the holiday while his Virginia contemporary Thomas Jefferson had little interest in the event. "The
holidays are barely mentioned in Jefferson's Christmas week
letters during his presidential years,"[1] notes social historian Alvin
Rosenbaum. James Polk worked on the holiday, and most other
nineteenth century presidents seemed relatively indifferent to any
public significance for Christmas.

Benjamin Harrison was the first Chief Executive to grant
a Christmas interview, giving one to a New York journalist in
1891. Ruminating on the religious and social meaning of the
holiday, he observed, "Christmas is the most sacred religious
festival of the year and should be an occasion of general rejoicing
throughout the land, from the humblest citizen to the highest
official, who, for the time being, should forget or put behind him
his cares and annoyances, and participate in the spirit of sea-

sonable festivity."[2]

Theodore Roosevelt provoked an outcry when he banned Christmas trees from the White House as a conservationist measure, but he relented when convinced that his position was untenable. He also gave impromptu sermons at the Christmas Eve carol services at Christ Church in Oyster Bay, New York.[3] Woodrow Wilson showed a mild Presbyterian disdain for the festival by attending the theater or playing golf on Christmas, though he attended a carol service on Christmas Eve, 1916 at the Treasury Department. Warren Harding's sole Christmas contribution was his pardon of socialist leader Eugene Debs and two dozen other political dissidents on Christmas Day in 1921.[4]

It was President Calvin Coolidge who inaugurated the custom of a formal presidential statement in 1927. In that first Christmas message "to the American people" Coolidge was characteristically terse. "Christmas is not a time or a season, but a state of mind. To cherish peace and good will, to be plenteous in mercy is to have the real spirit of Christmas. If we think on these things, there will be born in us a Savior and over us will shine a star sending its gleam of hope to the world," he said.[5]

His successor Herbert Hoover was a man of few words. His Christmas messages were brief and rather ethereal.

By contrast, Franklin D. Roosevelt, the great communicator, made his messages warm and earthy. He made his audiences feel that he cared about them personally, despite depressions and wars. When World War II came, FDR let Americans know that his sons were fighting abroad, just like their sons. He and Eleanor missed them. Christmas would not quite be Christmas until all family members were reunited.

One of the most eloquent presidential Christmas messages was FDR's last, that of Christmas Eve, 1944. He said:

> It is not easy to say "Merry Christmas" to you, my fellow Americans, in this time of destructive war. Nor can I say "Merry Christmas" lightly tonight to our Armed Forces at their battle stations all over the world or to our allies who fight by their side.

Here, at home, we will celebrate this Christmas Day in our traditional American way because of its deep spiritual meaning to us; because the teachings of Christ are fundamental in our lives; and because we want our youngest generation to grow up knowing the significance of this tradition and the story of the coming of the immortal Prince of Peace and Good Will. But, in perhaps every home in the United States, sad and anxious thoughts will be continually with the millions of our loved ones who are suffering hardships and misery, and who are risking their very lives to preserve for us and for all mankind the fruits of His teachings and the foundations of civilization itself.

The Christmas spirit lives tonight in the bitter cold of the front lines in Europe and in the heat of the jungles and swamps of Burma and the Pacific islands. Even the roar of our bombers and fighters in the air and the guns of our ships at sea will not drown out the messages of Christmas which come to the hearts of our fighting men. The thoughts of these men tonight will turn to us here at home around our Christmas trees, surrounded by our children and grandchildren and their Christmas stockings and gifts just as our own thoughts go out to them, tonight and every night, in their distant places.

The Chief Executive pledged that "Christmases such as those we have known in these years of world tragedy shall not come again to beset the souls of the children of God." He prayed that "God will protect our gallant men and women" . . . and that "He will receive unto His infinite grace those who make their supreme sacrifice in the cause of righteousness, in the case of love of Him and His teachings." It was an unapologetically religious statement.

FDR's successor, Harry Truman, was also unashamedly religious in many of his Christmas messages. In an increasingly secular age, he was not afraid to proclaim Jesus "the Redeemer of the World" in his 1951 address. Nor did he hesitate to affirm in 1952, his last Christmas at the White House: "Through Jesus Christ the world will yet be a better and finer place. This faith sustains us today as it has sustained mankind for centuries past.

This is why the Christmas story, with the bright stars shining and the angels singing, moves us to wonder and stirs our hearts to praise." He concluded his Christmas message with these words: "I wish for all of you a Christmas filled with the joy of the Holy Spirit, and many years of future happiness with the peace of God reigning upon this earth."

Mr. Truman seemed to relish the preacher role in his Christmas messages. Also in 1952 he said: "The first Christmas was God's great gift to us. This is a wonderful story. Year after year it brings peace and tranquillity to troubled hearts in a troubled world. . . . As we go about our business of trying to achieve peace in the world, let us remember always to try to act and live in the spirit of the Prince of Peace."

Like his predecessor, Truman sought to link the Christmas promise of peace and good will to U.S. military efforts abroad. In 1951, he said: "Our hearts are saddened on this Christmas Eve by the suffering and the sacrifice of our brave men and women in Korea. They are protecting us, and all free men, from aggression. They are trying to prevent another world war."

That same year, Mr. Truman also expressed a sentiment shared by millions of his fellow countrymen: "Christmas is the great home festival. It is the day in all the year which turns our thoughts toward home. And so I am spending Christmas in my old home in Independence with my family and friends."

Dwight Eisenhower also waxed eloquent at Christmastide. And he had a practical side. His holiday remarks were often directed toward particular needs of particular segments of society.

In his last Christmas message in 1960, Ike issued an appeal to holiday motorists to exercise caution and patience to reduce the appalling holiday traffic death toll. And he urged Americans to wipe out "bitter prejudice" based on "differences in skin pigmentation." He concluded: "Christmas . . . impels us to test the sincerity of our own dedication to the ideals so beautifully expressed in the Christian ethic. We are led to self-examination. . . . As we look into the mirror of conscience, we see blots and blemishes that mar the picture of a nation of people who devoutly believe that they were created in the image of their Maker."

In 1956, shortly after the crises in the Suez and in Hungary, Eisenhower told his nationwide audience:

In this Nation's capital city we are joined tonight with millions in all our forty-eight States, and, indeed, throughout the world, in the happiness and in the hope that Christmas brings.

Not that everyone is filled with happiness and hope in this season of rejoicing. Far from it. There is weariness. There is suffering for multitudes. There is hunger as well as happiness, slavery as well as freedom in the world tonight. But in the myriads of Christmas candles we see the vision of a better world for all people.

In the light of Christmas, the dark curtains of the world are drawn aside for a moment. We see more clearly our neighbors next door; and our neighbors in other nations. We see ourselves and the responsibilities that belong to us. Inspired by the story of Christmas we seek to give of our happiness and abundance to others less fortunate. Even now the American people, on the farm and in the city, rallying through the Red Cross and other voluntary agencies to meet the needs of our neighbors in Hungary, are true to the spirit of Christmas.

Returning to his gentle, homiletic tone, the President concluded:

In the warm glow of the Christmas tree, it is easy to say these things, but when the trees come down and lights are put away as they always are then we have a true testing of the spirit. That testing will be answered, throughout the year ahead, by the success each of us experiences in keeping alive the inspiration and exaltation of this moment.

We must proceed by faith, knowing the light of Christmas is eternal, though we cannot always see it.

Eisenhower liked to issue special Christmas messages to such groups as the Boy Scouts, the U.S. Armed Forces, those in the merchant marine. In 1955 he sent a Christmas message to the people of Eastern Europe.

John F. Kennedy delivered only two Christmas messages. Eschewing the preaching or explicitly religious tone, Mr. Kennedy approached the tree-lighting ceremony as "an important responsibility," "a formal way of initiating the Christmas season."

In 1962 he noted how widespread the practice of Christmas celebrations had become.

> We mark the festival of Christmas which is the most sacred and hopeful day in our civilization. For nearly 2,000 years the message of Christmas, the message of peace and goodwill towards all men, has been the guiding star of our endeavors. This morning I had a meeting at the White House which included some of our representatives from far-off countries in Africa and Asia. They were returning to their posts for the Christmas holidays. Talking with them afterwards, I was struck by the fact that in the far-off continents Moslems, Hindus, Buddhists, as well as Christians, pause from their labors on the 25th day of December to celebrate the birthday of the Prince of Peace. There could be no more striking proof that Christmas is truly the universal holiday of all men. It is the day when all of us dedicate our thoughts to others; when all are reminded that mercy and compassion are the enduring virtues; when all show, by small deeds and large and by acts, that it is more blessed to give than to receive.

In 1961, President Kennedy told West Berliners in a special Christmas message that the "beacon of freedom in Berlin will continue to shine brightly for many years to come. We are at your side as before and we shall stay. Until truly there is goodwill among men, not walls to divide them, our pursuit of peace shall continue."

Lyndon Johnson, Richard Nixon, and Gerald Ford opted for low-key Christmas messages that tended to link the fortune of the nation with the spirit and mood of the holiday season.

Johnson had the sorrowful task of delivering his first Christmas remarks one month after the assassination of John Kennedy. The lighting of the Christmas tree represented the end of the thirty-day period of national mourning.

Mr. Johnson said:

> Tonight we come to the end of the season of great national sorrow, and to the beginning of the season of great, eternal joy. We mourn our great President, John F. Kennedy, but he would have us go on. While our spirits cannot be light, our hearts need not be heavy.
>
> We were taught by Him whose birth we commemorate that after death there is life. We can believe, and we do believe, that from the death of our national leader will come a rebirth of the finest qualities of our national life.
>
> We have our faults and we have our failings, as any mortal society must. But when sorrow befell us, we learned anew how great is the trust and how close is the kinship that mankind feels for us, and most of all, that we feel for each other. We must remember, and we must never forget, that the hopes and the fears of all the years rest with us, as with no other people in all history. We shall keep that trust working, as always we have worked, for peace on earth and good will among men."

Richard Nixon emphasized America's contributions to peace and good will and celebrated its achievements as a nation in his seasonal remarks. Peace was the touchstone of his 1969 address. He said:

> But above everything else in this Christmas season, as we open this Pageant of Peace and as we light this Nation's Christmas tree, our wish, our prayer, is for peace, the kind of peace that we can live with, the kind of peace that we can be proud of, the kind of peace that exists not just for now but that gives us a chance for our children also to live in peace.
>
> That is what we believe in. That is what Americans stand for and that, believe me, is what we shall have.
>
> And, my friends, I also say to you that as we look at this

great tree, there is an old saying about Christmas trees. It goes something like this: May a Christmas tree be as sturdy as faith, as high as hope, as wide as love. And I could add, may a Christmas tree, our Christmas tree, be as beautiful as peace.

I think it is. I think it will be. And may this moment be one that history will record as one in which America looked forward to a decade of the seventies in which we could celebrate our Christmases at peace with all the world.

Gerald Ford returned to the Hoover tradition of brief, understated messages. In 1974, for example, he said:

Mrs. Ford and I send our warmest holiday greetings to all our fellow citizens. We hope that each of you will share the traditional joys of this Holy Season with your family and friends. And we pray that the Christmas spirit of generosity and renewal will be with you throughout the coming year.

We begin 1975 in the midst of many serious challenges. As we work to resolve them, let us be encouraged by counting the blessings we have gained from those who have met similar challenges in the past. Let us draw strength from our unity of purpose and hope from our past resourcefulness. And let us work together to ensure that the good which we have achieved will be strengthened and preserved for our children and future generations.

Jimmy Carter, one of our most personally religious presidents, preferred the simple, direct touch. In 1979 he alluded to the hostage crisis, talked about nuclear disarmament, the pope's recent visit, and the Year of the Child. At his direction, the lights on the fifty small trees were to remain unlighted until, he said, "the American hostages come home." Only the "Star of Hope on the top of the great Christmas tree" was lighted. It was that year, also, that Mr. Carter lighted a menorah in Lafayette Park to honor the Jewish festival of Hanukkah.

Carter reminded his audience that year:

Christmas means a lot of things. It means love. It means warmth. It means friendship. It means family. It means joy. It means light. But everyone this Christmas will not be experiencing those deep feelings. At this moment there are fifty Americans who don't have freedom, who don't have joy, and who don't have warmth, who don't have their families with them. And there are fifty American families in this Nation who also will not experience all the joys and the light and the happiness of Christmas.

Ronald Reagan's 1981 address ranks with the messages of Roosevelt and Truman for its religious content. In his message he combined personal and universal elements, saying:

At Christmas time every home takes on a special beauty, a special warmth. That is certainly true of the White House, where so many famous Americans have spent their Christmases over the years. This fine, old home the people's house has seen so much, been so much a part of all our lives and history. It has been humbling and inspiring for Nancy and me to be spending our first Christmas in this place.

We've lived here as your tenants for almost a year now, and what a year it's been. As a people we've been through quite a lot, moments of joy, of tragedy, and of real achievement moments that I believe have brought us all closer together.

G. K. Chesterton once said that the world would never starve for wonders, but only for the want of wonder. At this special time of year we all renew our sense of wonder in recalling the story of the first Christmas in Bethlehem nearly two thousand years ago.

Some celebrate Christmas as the birthday of a great and good philosopher and teacher. Others of us believe in the divinity of the Child born in Bethlehem; that He was and is the promised Prince of Peace. . . .

Tonight, in millions of American homes, the glow of the Christmas tree is a reflection of the love Jesus taught us.

Like the shepherds and wise men of that first Christmas, we Americans have always tried to follow a higher light, a star, if you will. At lonely campfire vigils along the frontier, in the darkest days of the Great Depression, through war and peace, the twin beacons of faith and freedom have brightened the American sky. At times our footsteps may have faltered, but trusting to God's help we have never lost our way.

Just across the way from the White House stand the two great emblems of the holiday season a menorah, symbolizing the Jewish festival of Hanukkah, and the National Christmas Tree, a beautiful towering blue spruce from Pennsylvania.

Turning to a more somber subject, the President castigated the Soviet Union for its repression of the spirit of freedom in Poland, "a proud and ancient nation, a land of deep religious faith where Christmas has been celebrated for a thousand years."

Mr. Reagan requested that all Americans burn a lighted candle in their windows to demonstrate solidarity with the Polish people. He said:

Let the light of millions of candles in American homes give notice that the light of freedom is not going to be extinguished. We are blessed with a freedom and abundance denied to so many. Let those candles remind us that these blessings bring with them a solemn obligation an obligation to the God who guides us, an obligation to the heritage of liberty and dignity handed down to us by our forefathers, and an obligation to the children of the world, whose future will be shaped by the way we live our lives today.

The presidential Christmas message is usually a lofty personal religious statement, which seems to fall under the protection of the free exercise clause. It has not raised some of the objections that another presidential ceremony, the lighting of the National Christmas Tree, has.[6]

Calvin Coolidge inaugurated the lighting of "the National Community Christmas Tree" in 1923. The reasons for it were completely secular. The electric companies wanted to encourage electric lights on Christmas trees. (So did insurance companies, since so many fires occurred as a result of lighted candles.) Frederick M. Feiker, an adviser to then Secretary of Commerce Herbert Hoover, urged Mr. Coolidge to set an example by lighting a tree donated by Middlebury College in the President's home state of Vermont. Coolidge agreed but refused to say a word for NBC Radio, which broadcast the ceremony. The President did agree to push the button.

The ceremony soon came to have a life of its own. Each year the crowds were greater, the music more lavish. Motorists blew their horns, the U.S. Marine Band played hymns and carols, the President spoke, and NBC broadcast the proceedings far and wide. The hapless tree, however, had a hard time finding a permanent home. It was on Sherman Square from 1924 to 1933, then in Lafayette Park from 1934 to 1938. After two years on the Ellipse, it was moved to the South Lawn of the White House in 1941, where it remained until 1953. Winston Churchill made a surprise appearance at the 1941 ceremony, just two weeks after the bombing of Pearl Harbor. For national security reasons it was lighted in neither 1942 nor 1943, but the ceremony was continued.

President Truman showed little interest in the event and did not even appear in 1948, 1949, or 1951. He wanted to be home in Independence, Missouri, on Christmas Eve, the traditional time for the ceremony. A popular Dwight Eisenhower gave the occasion a new lease on life in 1953.

Then, in 1954, a nonprofit corporation called the Christmas Pageant of Peace, Inc., with a permanent office at 1616 K Street in Washington, D.C., was established to make the annual event the kind of extravagant undertaking beloved of Americans in those days. The ceremony now lasted for 15 days or more. A life-sized Nativity scene was erected. The event was televised nationally, and all the activities were now held on the Ellipse, formerly the "President's Park." While private funds were largely responsible for the ceremonies, there was enough government involvement, through the Interior Department and the National Park Service, to suggest government sponsorship.

The event's organizers saw it as nonsectarian. They said,

"'The Pageant of Peace is a voluntary expression of American citizens of every creed and race to dramatize the Christmas Message 'Peace on Earth, Good Will Toward Men.' It is organized to foster friendship and understanding among all peoples; to reflect the unity of purpose that emanates from the diversity of traditions and backgrounds of mankind." The annual event soon took on the trappings of "civil religion" at its best (or worst). The event now symbolized for many the religious basis of American democracy in contrast with our deadly enemy, godless Communism. It symbolized the yearning for peace.

It was a visible representation of what historian William Lee Miller labeled "piety on the Potomac" during the Eisenhower years. It was at this time that a National Day of Prayer was mandated by Congressional action, and the phrase "under God" was added to the Pledge of Allegiance. The genial and immensely popular President saw religion as an essential component, even an ally, of his government. Eisenhower initiated the annual Presidential Prayer Breakfast, began cabinet meetings with prayer, and even composed his own prayer for his 1953 Inauguration, shortly after which he was baptized into the Presbyterian Church. The Christmas Pageant of Peace has to be seen in the context of a renewed public religiosity.[7]

While these ceremonies continued under Kennedy, Johnson and Nixon, it was the inclusion of the Nativity scene, or creche, that brought forth the next controversy.

In 1969 the American Civil Liberties Union brought suit in federal court, contending that including a creche in a government-sponsored event on government property violated the First Amendment ban on establishment of religion. Three of the plaintiffs were clergy persons, including Father William Wendt, pastor of the Episcopal Church of St. Stephen and the Incarnation. Others included Edward L. Ericson, of the American Ethical Union, and co-founder of Americans for Religious Liberty. The pageant sponsors, who had an exclusive permit from the Interior Department for all events on the Ellipse, countered that the Nativity scene was a "reminder of our spiritual heritage." A strange comment came from Assistant U.S. Attorney General Gil Zimmerman, who replied that the creche is not intended as a religious symbol.[8] The U.S. Court of Appeals refused to halt the creche until a three-judge panel could examine the case (*Allen v. Hickel*) on its merits.[9]

The case dragged on and on. Finally, in September, 1973, the case, now called *Allen* v. *Morton,* was settled. After having been initially thrown out at the District Court level for lack of jurisdiction, the Court of Appeals reversed and remanded the case to the District Court for a hearing on the merits. The U.S. Court of Appeals ruled that the creche either had to be dropped from the pageant or the government had to end its role in the display in order to limit a constitutionally impermissible "excessive entanglement" between government and religion.

The appellate court was convinced that the pageant had stepped over the line separating church and state. The Ellipse was also held to be government property, since it belongs to the White House. The court suggested that a creche could be acceptable if a private group applied for a permit on an equal basis with other groups and erected the creche on the Mall, a large grassy area extending from the Capitol to the Lincoln Memorial. The Mall has been held to be an open public forum, where a variety of political and religious expressions are welcome. This Court decision sought a Solomonic compromise, but was widely disliked by conservative Christians and others.[10]

For the next decade a private group called the American Christian Heritage Association erected a creche on the Mall. A zealous Marylander, Vaughn Barkdoll, director of public works for Prince George's County, established the group as a result of his disappointment with the court ruling. He appealed for private donations and for help from the Knights of Columbus.[11] In 1978 the Christian Service Corps began the National Christmas Nativity Drama on the grounds of the Washington Monument on the Mall. Ironically, a minor dispute in 1978 resulted in further legal action in which Federal District Court Judge William T. Bryant required the National Park Service to allow the private group access to the Mall.[12]

This solution seemed to satisfy most people, but in 1984 the Reagan Administration, which saw itself as the great defender of religion in American life, quickly moved to return a creche to the official Pageant of Peace ceremony on the Ellipse. This was in response to the recently announced Supreme Court decision in the Lynch v. Donnelly case. Officials based their decision on the High Court's holding in favor of a municipally sponsored creche in Pawtucket, Rhode Island. An activist group called Citizens for God and Country in McLean, Virginia lobbied for the action and called the Park Service decision "an unbelievable achievement" that will "serve the moral order" of the world. Jewish, Episcopal, Lutheran and Unitarian Universalist groups urged Interior Secretary William P. Clark to forbid a display until the High Court ruled in another creche case from Scarsdale, New York.[13]

After the rather unusual Scarsdale ruling, which will be discussed later, opponents of religious symbols in the federally sponsored event tried one last effort: an appeal to fair play and reason. Joel Levy spoke on behalf of several Jewish organizations and urged the National Park Service not to "give offense" to Americans "who adhere to non-Christian traditions." Levy reminded the Park Service, "Whether or not it is constitutionally permissible to include a creche (or religious symbol of any faith) in the Pageant, its inclusion certainly is not constitutionally required." Levy also said, "For some Americans who are not Christians—American Jews, Moslems, Hindus and Buddhists— the inclusion of the creche in the pageant is perceived as an indication that they are, at least to this extent, less than fully equal. For some Christians, inclusion of a creche in a secular Christmas pageant borders on sacrilege."[14]

The Park Service ignored the requests. A creche now appears each year.

Another arena of contention was the U.S. Postal Service. Religiously oriented stamps were considered unacceptable for most of American history. But in recent years the commission hearing requests from the Citizens Advisory Committee has approved of stamps honoring St. Francis of Assisi, Martin Luther, Father Junipero Serra and other religious figures.

In 1962 Postmaster General J. Edward Day issued the first U.S. Christmas stamp, which included candles and wreaths. There was no opposition until 1966 when a distinctly religious stamp featuring a Madonna and Child appeared as the official U.S. stamp. Americans United for Separation of Church and State criticized this decision as government preference for one religion. The postal authorities ignored the protest. Several more religious stamps were issued. Americans United filed suit in federal court, but the court rejected the contention.[15]

In *Americans United* v. *O'Brien*, the U.S. District Court for the District of Columbia issued its opinion on September 14, 1967, saying, in part, "The publication of a postage stamp, even if it consists of a design of religious significance, is outside of the ban of the two restrictions on the powers of government. It cannot be deemed in any sense even remotely connected with an establishment of religion, or with any limitation of the free exercise thereof."[16] The organization's appeal of this ruling was also rejected.

As a compromise of sorts, the Postal Service began issuing a religious stamp and a secular stamp for Christmas, 1970. They are now called "traditional" and "contemporary" stamps.

In 1987 the Postal Service unveiled its religious stamp in an unusual ceremony at the National Gallery of Art in Washington, D.C. To celebrate a sixteenth-century Italian Madonna and Child stamp by Giovanni Moroni, a sixth-grade ensemble from St. Peter's Interparish School was invited to participate in the October 23 inauguration ceremony and sing Christmas carols. During the ceremony, the Rev. Raymond Boland, vicar general and chancellor of the Catholic Archdiocese of Washington, sought divine approval for the new stamp. He prayed, "Bless us as we issue a new stamp. Yes, Lord, a new stamp. If the Holy Mother and Your Son look Italian, don't blame Moroni, because he didn't get to Palestine too often."

Adding a touch of ecumenism, the Rev. Edison Amos of the

Potomac United Methodist Church gave the benediction for the event.[17]

The presidents and the Postal Service are not the only sponsors and supporters of public Christmas celebrations. The "Community Christmas Tree" movement, which seems to have begun in Pasadena, California, in 1909, has helped to foster substantial public support for the holiday.

Residents of Pasadena decorated a large evergreen tree with electric lights on top of Mount Wilson in 1909. Not to be outdone, New York City residents erected a Tree of Light at the first Madison Square Garden, on 25th Street and Fifth Avenue, in 1911. It attracted large crowds, and in 1913 a community tree was erected at City Hall.

Boston mounted a display on the famed Commons in 1912, and Philadelphia followed suit with a tree on Independence Square in 1913. By 1914 over three hundred cities had community festivals. The small town of Altadena, California, created a lavish display along "Christmas Tree Lane" in 1920.

The involvement of local civil officials and the expenditure of public tax funds varied from community to community. Private commercial interests were also intimately involved in promoting ever more lavish Christmas activities. The Rockefeller Center Christmas tree began modestly in 1931 when local construction workers set up a small tree on the site of the new RCA Building. Two years later a formal tree lighting ceremony was inaugurated, and a choir from Columbia University participated. The tree lighting ceremony became nationally known over network radio, and, in 1951, was broadcast on national television as part of the "Kate Smith Show."[18]

Another popular tree was the General Grant sequoia tree, a 267-foot tall resident of the King's Canyon National Park in California. President Calvin Coolidge designated the tree the "Nation's Christmas Tree" on April 28, 1926. Each Christmas Day a ceremony, including music and prayer, is held at this federally maintained park.[19]

The Community Christmas celebration movement, which

even had a permanent office called "Tree of Light" in New York City, had many aims. At least one of them was inappropriate. In his admirable study, The Modern Christmas in America, William B. Waits says that the community organizers "wanted to promote religious homogeneity in cities."[20] Continuing, he writes, "Although organizers refrained from stating this goal explicitly, it was an important motivation for their promotion of the festivals. It prompted them to select Christmas as the occasion for community festivals, and to make Christian symbols, such as manger scenes and stars atop the Christmas trees, prominent at the celebrations. Entertainment always included the singing of Christmas carols and hymns."[21]

Waits argues that this underlying goal was counterproductive to interfaith harmony. "The liberal use of Christian symbols at community celebrations was an affront to the non-Christian residents, who felt they could not participate equally and felt less favored. In generating these negative feelings, the use of Christian symbols contradicted an important festival goal: strengthening the identification of all urban residents with their cities, regardless of religious or other preferences."[22]

Public officials, especially mayors and governors, have used Christmas as occasions of promoting good will in their communities. Tree-lighting ceremonies on municipal property and on state capitol complexes have become commonplace.

Finally, one federal agency gave Christmas some additional support in 1951. That year, the National Labor Relations Board ruled that employers who had customarily presented Christmas bonuses to their workers could not stop doing so by claiming they were voluntary gifts from management.[23]

Notes

1. Alvin Rosenbaum, A White House Christmas (Washington, D.C.: The Preservation Press, 1992), p. 38.
2. See Albert J. Menendez, Christmas in the White House (Phila-

delphia: Westminster Press, 1983), p. 111.

3. Ibid., p. 11.

4. Rosenbaum, pp. 113–14.

5. Coolidge's statement is found in the Calvin Coolidge room at the Northampton, Massachusetts, Public Library. All other Presidential Christmas messages from Herbert Hoover to George Bush are located in the *Public Papers of the Presidents,* an annual publication of the U.S. Government Printing Office since 1929.

6. Menendez, pp. 111–12.

7. Ibid., pp. 39–52.

8. *Houston Chronicle,* December 14, 1969, p. 12.

9. 424 F.2d 944 (D.C. Circuit 1970).

10. *Allen v. Morton,* 495 F.2d 65 (D.C. CIrcuit 1973).

11. Leon Wynter, "Watching Over the Nativity," *Washington Post,* December 25, 1980, pp. 5–6.

12. Religious News Service, November 27, 1978.

13. *Church & State* 38 (January 1985): p. 3.

14. Statement, Joel H. Levy, on behalf of the American Jewish Congress, National Jewish Community Relations Advisory Council, and Synagogue Council of America before the National Park Service, November 1, 1985.

15. Gaston D. Cogdell, "Religion and the Post Office," *Church & State* 20 (January 1967): pp. 11–12. See also *Church & State* 19 (September 1966): p. 23.

16. *Church & State* 20 (November 1967): pp. 14–15.

17. *Church & State* 40 (December 1987): p. 16.

18. Jack Maguire, *O Christmas Tree!* (New York: Avon, 1992), pp. 33–42.

19. Ibid., pp. 48–51.

20. William B. Waits, *The Modern Christmas in America* (New York: New York University Press, 1993), p. 155.

21. Ibid.

22. Ibid.

23. Ibid., pp. 188–89.

6

The December Dilemma
in the Public Schools

Can religious Christmas carols, songs and hymns be sung during public school assemblies? What about secular ditties, extolling the virtues of Santa Claus and Frosty the Snowman? Can Christmas parties be held, gifts exchanged, trees and evergreens erected in classrooms and hallways? These are just a few of the questions that thousands of public school teachers, principals and boards have to resolve each year as the days grow shorter, the weather colder and the 25th of December nears.

The dilemmas today are largely a result of increasing sensitivity toward religious minorities, the undeniable pluralism of U.S. society, and the greater scrutiny of the courts in enforcing Constitutional provisions for church-state separation. It was not always so difficult a task.

America's public schools generally reflected local religious conditions. That is, they were usually Protestant in tone, despite the existence of substantial numbers of Catholic and Jewish students.

Christmas in the schools tended to follow the increasing legal, commercial and religious acceptability of the holiday.

Ohio and California enacted laws before the Civil War ended, making Christmas a public school holiday. Many states followed suit in the 1890s so that by 1931 forty-one states had laws requiring the dismissal of public school children on December 25.[1] In the other seven states it was customary to do so. Generally, a period of one or two weeks vacation became the norm.

Disputes soon arose over the nature of the celebration and the degree of religiousness. In mostly Christian areas, which includes most of the country, the public schools celebrated Christmas with a full panoply of music and festivities, usually with a strong religious content.

Jews and other religious minorities, including those Christians who do not recognize the holiday, were left out.

One of the least-known incidents in American history took place in New York in 1906, when thousands of Jewish pupils boycotted the public schools to protest obligatory Christian religious assemblies at Christmastime. Here is what happened.

In December 1905 Fred F. Harding, principal of P.S. 144, an elementary school in the predominantly Jewish Brownsville district of Brooklyn, exhorted his students at a Christmas assembly "to be more like Christ." He had been doing this for years, and Jewish parents were fed up. A petition asking for his dismissal was presented to the local school board. Harding was accused of establishing "a policy of systematically Christianizing children born and raised in the Jewish faith . . . and for that purpose has at various times conducted quasi-religious services in the assembly room of his school." However, the local board exonerated the principal and ignored the evidence. The problem was acute throughout the New York City school system.

The next year Jewish representatives petitioned the school board to abolish "the singing of denominational hymns, the writing of compositions on subjects of religious character, the holding of festivities in which clergymen make speeches and the use of the Christmas tree." A Methodist delegation demanded that the exercises be continued. The school board dragged its feet and refused to act. A united Jewish community decided to act.

Leonard Bloom tells what happened next. "Subsequent actions of the school authorities led to increasing anxiety in the Jewish community. The climax came . . . with an emotionally charged and highly effective citywide boycott of pre-Christmas classes by Jewish pupils."[2]

The 1906 strike was successful, Bloom says, "in terms of the number of children involved, its broad coverage in the press, its immense effect on school personnel, and the change in Board of Education policy that it produced."[3]

By the time Christmas came around again, in 1907, the schools had removed all of the explicitly religious activities, leaving only Santa Claus and Christmas trees. The Jewish community finally felt at home in the tax-supported schools of the most Jewish city in the world.

The problem recurred after the Second World War. The Rabbinical Assembly of America issued this statement in 1946: "Christmas may have many general folk elements which are popular with children. But sincere and thoughtful Christians will surely agree that Christmas is primarily a religious festival. . . . The practice of calling on Jewish children to join in the singing of Christmas carols, to take part in Christmas plays . . . must be regarded as an infringement on their rights as Americans."[4] The Central Conference of American Rabbis counseled Jewish parents to forbid their children's participation in these activities but urged them not to make formal objections.[5] Still, the pressures to conform were intense.

Writing in the *Reconstructionist* in 1948, Abraham Segal stated bluntly, "Christmas confronts a Jewish child with unfair, difficult choices."[6] He cited peer pressure, and the conflicts arising within the family. While expressing reluctance to challenge the Christian majority, he asserted, "If one child in a school is Jewish out of a thousand who are not, the thousand still have no right to make the one suffer in conscience."[7] A number of Jews accepted the status quo, and some have always celebrated the secular aspects of the holiday.[8]

Most Christians, however well-intentioned, seemed uninterested in these pleas. James Barnett observed in 1954:

> Christmas observance in the public schools is accepted without question by most Christians, and a direct challenge to the legitimacy of the practice appears absurd to many. However, Jews are on strong logical ground in objecting to such ceremonies in public schools because there is no doubt that even the folk attributes of Christmas are embedded in a matrix of beliefs and customs related to Christianity. Furthermore, some of the folk symbols have acquired a semi-religious meaning through long association with nativity accounts.[9]

Even the slightest protest is likely to upset community harmony and inflame passions. Leonard Gross, a senior editor at *Look* magazine, described what happened in the seemingly enlightened town of Boulder, Colorado, home of the University of Colorado, in the early 1960s:

> A mixed group of Boulder residents protested to the city's school board that Christmas observances had become so excessive they seemed to endorse one religious position; decorations had become so elaborate that one Christian, on entering a school auditorium, felt compelled to genuflect. The school board found merit in the complaints and agreed to cut back. What was educational or cultural would remain. What was religious or worshipful would be removed.
>
> Most teachers accepted the order. Some, however, became so enraged that they ripped down Christmas decorations in front of their classes and announced that there would be no Christmas at all in the schools. That afternoon, many of the children went home crying. For the next week, the Boulder *Camera* carried outraged letters from parents. Shortly thereafter, a hastily summoned school-board meeting drew 1,000 parents, most of them angry, a few frightened.
>
> Even today, eyewitnesses recall that meeting with awe. "A mob response," says one. "The mood of the Crucifixion," says

another. When Larry Weiss, soft-spoken editorial writer for the Denver *Post*, pleaded, "Without minority rights, there can be no majority rights," he was hooted down. For weeks after the meeting, the Jews lived in fear. One, the wife of a University of Colorado professor, received a phone call: "If you know what's good for you, get out of town." A cross burned on the school superintendent's lawn; the following year, the president of the school board refused to seek reelection.[10]

Some Christians saw the retention of nativity scenes as a front-line of defending their way of life. They saw no constitutional objections. Indeed, one legal challenge to a creche on a public school lawn failed in 1958. A creche had been erected in 1956 on the lawn at Ossining Junior-Senior High School, in a New York City suburb. Twenty-eight Ossining residents objected on grounds of church-state separation. The school board said the display merely depicted "an historical event." Judge Elbert T. Gallagher of the Westchester County Supreme Court upheld the display but ruled that the creche could only be erected when school was not in session. This was one of the rare defeats for eminent constitutional scholar Leo Pfeffer, who argued the plaintiffs' case. Undoubtedly the decision represented the temper of the times.[11]

A few Christians recommended change to school boards in the 1960s. One representative example was Robert K. Menzel, chairman of the religion department at Concordia College in Portland, Oregon. He challenged the school's celebration of distinctively religious events, saying:

Neither children nor public schools, neither church nor public benefits from the traditional forms of Christmas holiday observance. . . . Moreover, typical Christmas observances in schools tend toward indoctrination and degenerate into meaningless ritual; weaken the witness of the church when it surrenders its peculiar functions to any agency of the state; and puts the public school into competition with the church.[12]

He also suggested that schools could teach about Christmas in art and music classes, if there were true curricular value. He said:

> Public schools need not ignore Christmas. They do not lack the imagination to utilize legitimate curricular and cocurricular means to change a troublesome event into a valuable educational experience. Gian Carlo Menotti's "Amahl and the Night Visitors" can be staged, Handel's oratorios presented, special art projects and displays arranged, appropriate units in literature and history scheduled to coincide with the season. There are abundant resources for classes in drama, music, literature, art, history, and social studies to make use of the Christmas season in a proper and profitable way.[13]

Menzel, a Lutheran pastor, also challenged those churches which insisted on religious activities. "As for the churches, if they can't provide programs and activities meaningful enough to bring the neighborhood children and parents voluntarily to 'come and adore Him,' why should they expect the coercive power of the school to get them to kneel at the manger?" he wrote.[14]

Most schools tended to do what they had always done, though some had begun introducing Hanukkah celebrations in the 1940s as a way of easing interfaith tensions. As we shall see, this is not widely acceptable to the Jewish community.

The December dilemma in the public schools since the 1970s has emerged as a result of two competing forces: the increasing religious and cultural pluralism of U.S. society and the desire of conservative Christians to reassert their influence over the nation's public life, culture, and educational institutions. This conflict, which has led to legal battles over the religious content of textbooks and religious observances in classroom settings and athletic events, shows no signs of abating. Communal strife and ill feelings along religious lines frequently mar the educational landscape as each winter holiday season draws closer.

During the 1970s at least three school boards and one important denomination adopted policy statements on the Christmas-in-the-schools question that are worthy of note and discussion.

In 1974 the Board of Education in Ithaca, New York, adopted nine guidelines to help school administrators resolve the long-standing controversy. They were developed through a process of careful consultation with community leaders. A multifaith advisory committee spent five months of discussions and study. This is the result:

> Resolved, that the Ithaca City School District will remain impartial with regard to religion.
>
> 1) The students, faculty and administration are reminded of the pluralism of religious beliefs. Specifically, that which is important and meaningful to some may be offensive and repugnant to others. Each person is reminded to be conscious of and respect the sensitivities of others.
>
> 2) Factual and objective teaching about religion may occur in the Ithaca City School System. Religious indoctrination is never appropriate in the public schools and is not supported by the Board of Education. Teachers may explain the meaning of religious holidays but may not recognize such holidays with religious observances in the classroom or in any mandated teaching situation.
>
> 3) Discussion of morality, ethics and values is encouraged. The ultimate responsibility for this rests with the home. The role of the school is one of clarification and support of moral values and not of inculcation of a particular set of sectarian values.
>
> 4) Sacred religious readings shall be permitted for historical or literary instruction. Religious reading and prayer for other purposes is governed by State and Federal laws.
>
> 5) Neither instructional materials nor assembly programs shall be used to promote or encourage any views concerning religion or nonreligion.
>
> 6) No student shall be required to sing religious songs that promote the beliefs of a particular faith or are associated with a religious observance.
>
> 7) Religious music, as part of a secular program, or concert,

is permitted provided it is presented in other than a religious context and on a volunteer basis.

8) Any volunteer groups under the supervision of a teacher may perform or listen to any music of their choice regardless of religious or secular content. Volunteer groups might include: a) school bands or orchestras, b) instrumental groups or solo performances, c) choral groups or choirs, d) recordings, e) drama, f) impromptu, informal groups.

9) Spontaneous self expression in either music or art is neither restricted nor prohibited. School displays, such as murals of wise men, manger scenes, Hanukkah menorah, crosses or crucifixes, Star of David, and the crucifixion scene, which promote religious observances are deemed inappropriate.[15]

The Long Island (New York) Interfaith Council issued some guidelines in 1978. They observed, "The public school should be religiously neutral. By this is meant not only that the school should show no preference for one religion over another but also that it should refrain from the promotion of any and all religions. Consequently, no religious holiday celebrations should be held in the public schools."

The guidelines define "religious celebration" as:

1) A worship or religious service of any kind, regardless of whether or not conducted by a clergyman.

2) Religious exhibits or displays, except to the extent that such display is a necessary or integral part of the study of some subject in the curriculum: e.g., art, history, etc., and with no intent to indoctrinate.

3) The presentation of religious music, except to the extent that such music is presented for its musical content only, rather than as a devotional exercise.

The guidelines also took the position that "the substitution of the 'winter season' celebration for a religious observance is a profanation and secularization of what truly is a period of religious significance for Christians and Jews."[16] The Long

Islanders also emphasized this point: "Teaching in the public schools may take cognizance of the fact that religious holidays are observed differently by different religious groups. Such teaching, if presented, should be factual and not devotional, and avoid any doctrinal impact or an implication that religious doctrines on which such holidays are based have the support of state authority."[17]

The education department of the state of Massachusetts also distributed a set of guidelines that year which stated that while the importance of religion in history and culture should have a place in education, the definition of what is appropriate is determined by whether the purpose or effect tends to advance a religious objective. Massachusetts educators were cautioned about singing Christmas carols for purely devotional reasons.[18]

The 175th General Assembly of the United Presbyterian Church in the United States grappled with this question and recommended this course of action:

The Special Committee on Church and State *recommends* that: (a) Churches recognize the administration of religious training and observance as the domain of church and family. (b) United Presbyterians actively strive to recapture from popular custom the observance of religious holidays in order to restore their deepest religious meaning. (c) Since the association of seasonal activities with religious holidays in the public schools tends to pervert their religious significance, such association be discouraged as foreign to the purpose of the public school. (d) Religious holidays be acknowledged and explained, but never celebrated religiously, by public schools or their administrators when acting in an official capacity. (e) Whenever possible, students of various religious faiths should be allowed sufficient time to permit the celebration of their religious observances away from public school property. (f) Religious observances should never be held in a public school or introduced into the public school as part of its program.[19]

While these concerns were translated into more harmonious relationships in some communities, the absence of such policies and the weight of history and tradition brought conflict to numerous others.

In North Carolina, a state where many schoolroom religious practices have continued in violation of Supreme Court decisions,[20] a human relations group in the state's capital city urged sensitivity on the part of the schools toward religious activities.

In 1973 the Raleigh Community Relations Commission asked that "public school programs and practices be kept as free as possible of all specifically religious connotations." The group adopted the resolution after some Jewish students complained that they were being required to participate in school Christmas programs. At another school, academic class time was used for decorating Christmas trees.

Reaction in the community was mixed. Several principals said students could elect to absent themselves from Christmas assembly programs, which, of course, misses the point. The U.S. Supreme Court specifically rejected this option in its school-prayer and Bible-reading decisions, noting that this singled out students for abuse because of their religious faith. The assistant superintendent of Raleigh schools, Stuart Thompson, huffed that the Commission's resolution "could demand repression of legitimate school activities and might lead to the elimination of all religious influences on the curriculum." He did admit that public schools should avoid proselytizing and that school assemblies should not become religious services. Several members of the school board dismissed the complaints as "far-fetched," "childish" and "asinine."[21]

A dispute in South Dakota's largest city, Sioux Falls, eventually led to the major court case regarding the singing of carols in the schools. In that heavily Christian town every public school held a religious Christmas assembly where generally half or more of the songs performed were religious in nature. In the elementary schools, religious allegories, plays and symbols were common practice. The area ACLU director, Stephen L. Pevar, commented:

In many schools, the Christmas assembly is the single most important event of the year with the exception of graduation. More time is spent on planning, rehearsing and performing the Christmas assembly than is spent on any other program. In Sioux Falls, choral groups begin rehearsing the Christmas program on October 1, which means that students are singing religious hymns during a third of their school year.[22]

The Sioux Falls Board of Education appointed a study committee to recommend policy after a local resident, Roger R. Florey, who is an atheist, objected to his son's participation in ceremonies that were to him religious indoctrination. When the board unanimously voted to continue religious carols in school programs, Florey and five other taxpayers asked the American Civil Liberties Union to represent them in a First Amendment lawsuit, which was filed in federal district court on November 30, 1978.[23] The district court ruled against the plaintiffs on February 14, 1979, observing that "prudent" use of religious materials was acceptable because even religious materials "have been assimilated into our culture."[24] The court admitted that the issue was a "close" case but said the school board "guidelines" were constitutional if "properly administered."[25]

At issue was a set of guidelines of recommended action for the 21 schools in Sioux Falls. The guidelines adopted were these:

1) The several holidays throughout the year which have a religious and a secular basis may be observed in the public schools. 2) The historical and contemporary values and the origin of religious holidays may be explained in an unbiased and objective manner without sectarian indoctrination. 3) Music, art, literature and drama having religious themes or basis are permitted as part of the curriculum for school-sponsored activities and programs if presented in a prudent and objective manner and as a traditional part of the cultural and religious heritage of the particular holiday. 4) The use of religious symbols such as a cross, menorah, crescent, Star of David, creche, symbols of Native American religions or other symbols that are a part

of a religious holiday is permitted as a teaching aid or resource provided such symbols are displayed as an example of the cultural and religious heritage of the holiday and are temporary in nature. Among these holidays are included Christmas, Easter, Passover, Hanukkah, St. Valentine's Day, St. Patrick's Day, Thanksgiving and Halloween.

At a hearing in the federal district court on December 7, 1978, the plaintiffs contended that the guidelines had a religious purpose and pointed to the 21 Christmas programs planned for later that month. The suit charged that the effect of the guidelines is to advance the majority religion in the community. Despite the fact that Hanukkah, a Jewish holiday cited for observance in the guidelines, fell on the same day as Christmas in 1978, only two of the 21 holiday programs in the schools included a song about Hanukkah and none contained Hanukkah plays or symbols. Three ministers testified that the school Christmas observances which included religious hymns and carols, stories and plays were indistinguishable from church services.

Plaintiffs also argued that the guidelines would unconstitutionally entangle government with religion by forcing school personnel to choose which religious material to use in holiday programs. The suit charged that the school programs go far beyond the teaching "about" religion which would be constitutionally acceptable.[26]

The plaintiffs appealed the decision to the Eighth Circuit Court of Appeals in St. Louis. The ACLU brief blasted the district court decision. Its most telling paragraph was this one:

With all due respect to the district court, its holding is the epitome of ethnocentrism. To the millions of non-Christians who live in this country, "our" culture is not their culture and they have not "assimilated" religious Christmas carols. Most people take their religion far too seriously to look upon religious songs as forms of art only. The day "Silent Night" is sung in Buddhist temples and Jewish synagogues throughout the United States is the day "Silent Night" will have been assimilated into "our" culture.

"Silent Night" is a religious song. It has achieved a degree of "secular and artistic significance" to be sure. But it is still a religious song which is why Christians sing it only in December. Only Christians have assimilated "Silent Night."[27]

Plaintiffs, including the American Jewish Congress, reminded the court of something Leo Pfeffer wrote some years ago in his classic book, *Church, State and Freedom:*

It is not a sufficient answer to say that the Jewish child need not join in the singing or the pageant if he does not want to. It is unfair and unconscionable to place on the child the burden of isolating himself from his classmates, to stand alone during the festivities and preparations for them which in many schools occupy practically all the school time in December.[28]

The impassioned ACLU brief also hit back at the common argument that if something has existed for a long time it must be okay. "Christmas assemblies might be a tradition in public school. But tradition does not take precedence over the Constitution. If it did, public schools would still be segregated and prayers would still be recited as a morning classroom exercise."[29]

The appellate court held the guidelines constitutional in April 1980, by a two to one vote. The appellate court also, like the lower court, did not address the specific programs springing from the guidelines the first year.

The majority opinion of the appellate court concluded:

The rules guarantee that material used has secular or cultural significance: Only holidays with both religious and secular basis may be observed; music, art, literature, and drama may be included in the curriculum only if presented in a prudent and objective manner and only as part of the cultural and religious heritage of the holiday; and religious symbols may be used only as a teaching aid or resource and only if they are displayed as part of the cultural and religious heritage of the holiday and are temporary in nature.

Since all programs and materials authorized by the rules must deal with the secular or cultural basis or heritage of the holidays and since the materials must be presented in a prudent and objective manner and symbols used as a teaching aid, the advancement of a "secular program of education," and not of religion, is the primary effect of the rules.

The appellate court cautioned that the guidelines should be carefully followed to avoid unconstitutional infringement on church-state separation. "The administration of religious training is properly in the domain of the family and church," the court said. "The First Amendment prohibits public schools from serving that function."[30]

On November 10 the Supreme Court declined to review this decision. While religious conservatives were generally pleased, many civil liberties groups took a dim view.

The *Florey* case really solved nothing on its own, though it remains the only federal appellate ruling relative to the carol controversy. As American Jewish Congress attorney Marc Stern noted, "As far as school boards are concerned, *Florey* is the last word."[31] School systems far and wide have tried to offer guidance to local schools without offending major segments of the community. It remains a genuine dilemma. Continuing to sing religious carols or music continues to offend the Jewish community and the growing Islamic, Buddhist and non-religious communities. But removal of all religious references, even those of a cultural nature, offends many Christians. A survey of several communities shows how difficult is has been:

• Even in Sioux Falls itself, some schools have eliminated Christmas observances and others began to tone down the religious content as early as 1981, according to the ACLU's Stephen Pevar.[32]

• Iowa's school celebrations vary widely. In larger, more religiously diverse communities like Des Moines, both the capital city and the most populous, religious music is kept to a minimum. Christmas trees are permitted but not encouraged and decorations must be nonreligious. A similar approach is taken in Cedar Rapids. In smaller towns, where everyone is nominally Christian, religious songs are included in school-sponsored activities.[33] In Iowa City, a sophisticated college town with some strong Catholic and Bible Belt antecedents, a debate about a strong religious emphasis in the Yuletide music program occurred in the early 1980s. Several principals wrestled with the issue, opting generally for "appropriateness" and "quality."[34]

• In Greensboro, North Carolina, community harmony was rattled in 1983 when a local black newspaper publisher, John Marshall Kilimanjaro, a convert to Judaism, objected to the strong religious content in the annual Christmas program at Mendenhall Junior High School. A half dozen Christmas and three Hanukkah songs were nixed. School Superintendent Kenneth Newbold agreed that including so many religious songs violated a 1980 school board policy against including materials offensive to any religious segment of the populace.

There was disappointment and anger, and a brief flurry of anti-Semitic nastiness at the school. In local newspaper columns a local teacher defended the performance as "a cultural event where there was no compulsory attendance or participation." Rabbi Edward H. Feldheim of the Beth David Synagogue emphasized that respect for religious values needed to be nurtured at home and in the churches and synagogues. He observed that while "it is important for all people to have knowledge about and appreciation for other religions, many of the Christmas and Hanukkah songs express deep religious beliefs that are not shared by all of us." The *Greensboro Daily News*, which opposes school prayer and other "obvious violations of the Establishment Clause," editorialized that "Christmas carols and Hanukkah songs have neutral connotations when sung in school concerts. They are not performed as part of a worship service but as part of an entertainment program." The paper also claimed that "although Christmas is a religious celebration for Christians, it is a cultural celebration for non-Christians."[35]

• An angry crowd of 500 parents and students jammed the Rochester, Minnesota, school administration building after the Board of Education barred Christmas trees, Nativity scenes, the singing of religious and secular carols, and appearances by Santa Claus. The Board said it was striving for neutrality. It, too, cited the *Florey* case, particularly the passage which said it was "inappropriate for schools to permit the celebration of religious holy days fostering a religious spirit." Many parents demanded a reversal of policy. An effigy of Santa Claus was hung outside the building, and one parent said the Board had "ruined Christmas" for many students.[36]

• Residents of Medford Township, New Jersey, found handbills in their mailboxes in the fall of 1982 which implied that Christmas was "being taken out of school." A large crowd showed up at a school board meeting to protest carefully drawn guidelines on religious holiday observance. With tears in her eyes, one parent said the board was "taking God out of the schools." Another woman said, "You have no fear of the Lord," while a third implied the devil was behind it. The Medford Board, responsible for five schools in south Jersey, had sought "to deal equitably with an increasingly pluralistic society where children come from a variety of religious backgrounds," explained school superintendent Robert M. Salati.[37]

• A music teacher at Salk Elementary School in Tulsa, Oklahoma, charged that removing religious songs or carols from the curriculum "could be psychologically damaging to students of the Christian faith." Rae Underwood threatened to initiate legal action to keep Christ in the classroom Christmas.[38]

• What may have been the most eccentric and charming potential Christmas case for the courts was the annual practice of a Rhode Island man, who visited local schools each December in the garb of St. Nicholas of Myra, the kindly fourth-century bishop who is a precursor of the Santa Claus legend. Lester York, a deacon at St. John the Evangelist Episcopal Church in Newport, began visiting public elementary schools during the late 1970s on December 6, the feast of St. Nicholas. York dressed the part. He wore green vestments, a bishop's mitre and carried a long copper crosier, or pastoral staff. Behind an imposing beard of white whiskers and twinkling eyes, York talked about the love of Jesus, peace and goodwill.

York said his presentations were ecumenical, because he explained the meaning of Hanukkah and the message of St. Basil to Greek children. He received the encouragement of both the Catholic and Episcopal bishops, and his visits also included local churches and parochial schools.

His defenders were many. Narrangansett principal David D. Hayes stoutly maintained that the visit was educational, not religious, because York talked about the fourth-century world, thus injecting historical material and complementing the school's social science curriculum.

But the religious message in a public school concerned Steven Brown, ACLU director, who labeled the visits "blatantly unconstitutional." "The Christian religion must be in a very sad state in Narrangansett if it needs to rely on the public schools to relay its message," he added. Brown asserted that York was "preaching and evangelizing while in the classroom. There is no question that he was expressing very particular Christian views." Brown added that there was a good possibility that his organization would file suit if a plaintiff could be found. York was charitable and a bit nonplussed by it all. "I've been in jail before," he said, "It was the year 325."[39] This contretemps ended in 1983 when the public schools withdrew their invitation to York, thereby avoiding a lawsuit.

• Schools in religiously diverse communities are not immune from controversy. In the Washington, D.C., suburb of Rockville,

Maryland, an overzealous teacher's aide at Rock Creek Valley Elementary School became incensed at the sight of a Christmas tree in the school's main office and promptly tossed it into the parking lot. Several students were aghast, and the aide's action became a local cause celebre. The tree was returned to its place. The school, where a significant percentage of the student body is Jewish, had been striving to implement a very enlightened Montgomery County policy on religious holidays. (Religious holidays are observed only as an academic study, not in a devotional or celebratory way, but some holiday symbols are allowed as examples of cultural heritage.)[40]

Some other Montgomery County residents objected to the inclusion of Hanukkah songs in elementary schools. (The county is 15 percent Jewish.) Both teachers and students in one school objected when the principal banned all Hanukkah and Christmas symbols in 1980.[41]

Across the Potomac River in Fairfax County, Virginia, an energetic fifth-grader organized her classmates at Laurel Ridge Elementary School after the principal announced that there would be no Christmas music or decorations in the school. The school was implementing a 1976 policy regulation stipulating that schools "should be neutral with respect to religion and shall not engage in any activity that advocates or disparages religion." This policy reflected the growing religious pluralism in this multi-ethnic, affluent county. Soon, complaints inundated the school board and the local human relations agency. Angry parents tried to work out a compromise in which Christmas and Hanukkah symbols were welcome. One parent dressed up as Santa Claus to make his point at an open meeting.[42]

The Pacific Coast states have also attempted to adjust to the proliferation of new religious movements and a changing school environment. Most Christmas programs are now relatively non-controversial.

In Oregon the state's attorney general, Lee Johnson, ruled in 1975 that public schools in Oregon may not permit Nativity scenes in school buildings while classes are being held. Johnson pointed out that the creche was "designed to emphasize the religious aspects of the Christmas season." Permission to hold Nativity scenes on the school property would imply sponsorship by the school district itself and would breach the principle of church-state separation. The issue arose in Portland in 1973 when a volunteer room-mother tried to take a Nativity scene to school but was prohibited from doing so by the school authorities. Her church protested to the Portland school board, which in turn appealed to the Oregon Board of Education and then to the attorney general.[43]

In Corvallis, site of Oregon State University, a new school board policy adopted in 1980 took some adjustment since many parents preferred the kind of traditional Christmas they remembered. The Corvallis policy carved out a strong distinction between teaching about religion and celebrating religious holidays. Religious holidays had to have an "instructional as opposed to devotional purpose" and "the activity cannot diminish, put at a disadvantage or discriminate against the religious beliefs of individuals or groups." The question of appropriate religious symbolism was left to local administrators and teachers, but the interference was clear that no overt symbols were allowable.[44]

Oregon state school officials advised their districts to be more judicious about the content of Christmas programs. The implementation was smooth, and even rural districts like Albany found ways to develop meaningful programs that were not offensive to segments of the community.[45]

In Washington State a superior court judge in Snohomish County ruled in 1986 that a creche and a menorah displayed in a public school classroom were unconstitutional. Judge Dennis Brett held that the display advanced the religious preference of the sponsoring teacher and his students. Brett invoked the federal Constitution's ban on Establishment of Religion. Brett held that enforcing a policy that allows a mixture of religious and nonreligious symbols required constant monitoring that will inevitably result in excessive entanglement between government and religion.

The dispute began the previous year when a science teacher at Olympia View Junior High School erected the symbols "to celebrate the birth of Christ." Mr. Gibson, an evangelical Protestant, said he was engaged in a "holy war between persons who believe in a personal relationship with Jesus Christ and those who do not."

Then parents filed suit to prevent a repetition of the incident. The teacher was popular, however, and a majority of students signed petitions and boycotted classes in support of the "right of the Christian majority to display religious symbols in the classroom."[46]

The decision was a low-level one. But Judge Brett made several strong points worth remembering in this whole religion-and-schools debate. He said, "The Supreme Court has continually been zealous in protecting the right of school children to be free from sectarian influence by school authorities. Thus, practices which may be acceptable for an adult audience or a public forum may be unacceptable for public schools where attendance is mandatory and the desire to conform is typical among youth of such age."[47] The local newspaper, The Herald, called the decision "welcome guidance" and a "reasonable message."[48]

The Christmas dilemma remains touchy in many school districts. In 1988 Boca Raton, Florida, school principal Susan Marshall allowed her Verde Elementary School pupils to sing only those religious songs included in state-adopted choral books. One Hanukkah song and one Christmas carol were allowed. (A committee of parents and teachers had recommended no religious music in classroom activities.) This compromise seemed to work. Across the country in Lee's Summit, Missouri, however, ninety-three public high school students skipped classes to protest a school board decision canceling an annual candle-lighting ceremony. They were suspended for three days. Uncertainty remains the norm, especially in school districts which have no firm policies regulating religious holiday observances.

A group of sixteen educational and religious groups formed a coalition to address these issues, and heralded their proposals as a solution. On October 5, 1989, at a Washington, D.C., press conference, the ad hoc group, which included the prestigious American Academy of Religion, the National Conference of Christians and Jews, the National Council of Churches, and the National Education Association, issued guidelines for perplexed school authorities.

The coalition encouraged school officials to approach religious holidays from an academic perspective and to avoid any promotion of religious beliefs or devotions. "There must be respect for people with strong religious beliefs and, at the same time, respect for those of other beliefs or no beliefs at all. A delicate balance needs to be struck in December and throughout the year," they concluded.

The role of teachers is crucial, the group maintained. "Teachers must be alert to the distinction between teaching *about* religious holidays, which is permissible, and *celebrating* religious holidays, which is not. On the touchy subject of religious music, they affirmed, "Sacred music may be sung or played as part of the academic study of music. School concerts that present a variety of selections may include religious music. Concerts should avoid programs dominated by religious music, especially when these coincide with a particular religious holiday."

As to Christmas specifically, the group issued this recommendation:

> Holiday concerts in December may appropriately include music related to Christmas and Hanukkah, but religious music should not dominate. Any dramatic productions should emphasize the cultural aspects of the holidays. Nativity pageants or portraying the Hanukkah miracle are not appropriate in the public school setting. None of the school activities in December should have the purpose, or effect, of promoting or inhibiting religion.

Holiday programs should "serve an educational purpose for all students" and should "make no students feel excluded or identified with a religion not their own."

This advice was praised by the *Washington Post,* which editorially commended the group's "straightforward" approach and "sensible" answers.[49]

Notes

1. James H. Barnett, *The American Christmas: A Study in National Culture* (New York: Macmillan, 1954), p. 66.

2. Leonard Bloom, "A Successful Boycott of the New York City Public Schools—Christmas 1906," *American Jewish History* 70 (December 1980): pp. 180-188.

3. Ibid. See also *The New York Times* for December 12, 1906; December 25, 1906; January 7, 1907; January 10, 1907; November 21, 1907; and December 25, 1907.

4. Ibid., p. 68.

5. Ibid.

6. Abraham Segal, "Christmas in the Public School," *Reconstructionist* 14 (Dec. 10, 1948): pp. 17-22.

7. Ibid.

8. Barnett, p. 68.

9. Ibid., p. 69.

10. Leonard Gross, "The Jew and Christmas," *Look* (December 28, 1965, pp. 12-14.

11. *Baer* v. *Kolmorgen,* 14 Misc. 2d 1015, 181, N.Y.S. 2d 230 (N.Y. Sup. Ct. 1958). See also Lee Orville Garber, "Christmas Creche May be Placed on School Grounds." *The Nation's Schools* 64 (December 1959): pp. 82-84.

12. Robert K. Menzel, "Should We Keep Christmas In Our Public Schools?" *Church & State* 19 (December 1966): pp. 8, 15.

13. Ibid.

14. Ibid.

15. *Church & State* 27 (December 1974): pp. 13-14. See also "Carol Question," and Robert L. Oakley, "The Carol Furor," in *Ithaca Journal,* October 8, 1974, pp. 16-17.

16. This information is found in "Religious Holiday Observances in Public Schools: A Guide for Community Action," published by the American Jewish Congress in 1978.

17. Ibid.

18. Ibid.

19. "Christmas in School," *Church & State* 32 (January 1979): p. 5.

20. See *Religion in the North Carolina Schools: the Hidden Reality*, a report published in 1983 by the North Carolina Project of People for the American Way.

21. Religious News Service, December 18, 1973.

22. Stephen L. Pevar, "Christmas Assemblies in the Public Schools," a paper prepared for a conference at Mount Vernon College in Washington, D.C. on June 16–19, 1979. Pevar was Regional Counsel of the ACLU Mountain States Regional office.

23. Religious News Service, December 11, 1978.

24. Ibid.

25. "Supreme Court Avoids Christmas Case," *Church & State* 33 (December 1980): pp. 10–11.

26. Ibid.

27. Pevar, p. 4.

28. Leo Pfeffer, *Church, State and Freedom* (Boston: Beacon Press, 1967), p. 490.

29. Pevar, p. 5.

30. 619 F 2d 1311 (8th Cir. 1980).

31. *School Law News*, December 17, 1982, p. 9.

32. Lucia Mouat, "Public Schools Face December Dilemma," *Christian Science Monitor*, December 9, 1981, p. 12.

33. Linda Lartor,"How Iowa Schools Handle Christmas Festivities," *Des Moines Register*, December 25, 1986.

34. Mouat, p. 1.

35. "Music at Mendenhall," *Greensboro Daily News*, December 17, 1983.

36. *Washington Post*, December 23, 1982. *Washington Times*, December 23, 1982.

37. *Philadelphia Inquirer*, November 14, 1982.

38. David L. Langford, "Move to Get Christ Out of Christmas Meets Resistance," *The Post-Crescent* (Appleton, Wisconsin), December 13, 1978.

39. Religious News Service, December 15, 1982; *School Law News*, December 17, 1982. See also Robert F. Baldwin, "Episcopalian Portrays St. Nick Over ACLU Objections," *Our Sunday Visitor*, December 26,

1982, p. 3.

40. *Washington Post,* December 18, 1979, pp. C1–C2. See also Clandette Sulton, "Holiday Spirit Sours in Church-State Protest," *Montgomery Sentinel,* December 20, 1979, pp. A17–A19.

41. Mike M. Ahlers, "Menorah, Nativity Display in Schools Stirring a Ruckus," *Montgomery Journal,* December 17, 1980, pp. A1, A13.

42. Denis Collins, "Schools Facing Christmas, Hanukkah Problem," *Washington Post,* December 1, 1979, p. B1, B4.

43. Religious News Service, July 31, 1975.

44. *Corvallis Gazette-Times,* November 27, 1981, p. 15.

45. "Schools Reflect Concern Over Church-State Issue," *Albany Democrat-Herald,* December 4, 1984.

46. *Mainger v. Mukilteo School District No. 6,* No. 85-2-0467102 (Superior Court of the State of Washington in and for the County of Snohomish) at 5.

47. Dale Folkerts, "Judge Rules Out Mukilteo School Religious Display," *The Herald,* November 10, 1986, p. 1.

48. "Ruling For Holiday Cheer," *The Herald,* November 12, 1986.

49. Rob Boston, "Resolving the December Dilemma," *Church & State* 42 (December 1989): pp. 4–7.

7

Creches, Menorahs, and Courts

The public display of Nativity scenes, or creches, has become the focal point in the modern legal controversies. The institution of the creche, or *presepio* in Italian, is often ascribed to St. Francis of Assisi, who celebrated Christmas in Greccio in 1224 with a full-scale Bethlehem scene. His biographers, including Thomas of Celano and Countess Martinego, have suggested that Francis wished to recreate the "haunting memories" he carried away from a visit to Bethlehem a few years earlier. This event was immortalized in a painting by Giotto.

However, historian Clement Miles says that the use of a visual tableau for Christmas can be traced back many centuries before Francis. Citing Usener and other historians, Miles says that the Roman Basilica of St. Mary Major was built by Pope Liberius as a special home to highlight the new Christmas festival. In the eighth century Pope Gregory III added to the elaborate ceremonies at St. Mary Major. An eleventh century liturgical drama called the *Officium Pastorum* included a presepio behind the altar.[1]

Cultural historian Francis X. Weiser also notes that the earliest known picture of a Nativity scene dates from the year 380 and was found as a wall decoration in a Christian family's tomb in St. Sebastian's Catacomb in Rome. It was discovered in 1877.[2]

Since the fourteenth century a veritable subcategory of folk art has been devoted to the creation of Nativity scenes, many of which are artistic masterpieces of their genre, especially the Neapolitan creches. Several European cultures have contributed to this popular art form, including the Moravian *putz*, an early and rare form of Protestant artistry. The American Southwest has contributed its *nacimientos* to the genre. Various medieval religious plays added to the popular devotions.

The little town of Pawtucket, Rhode Island, seems an unlikely place for a major church-state confrontation, one that reached the nation's highest court in a decision which has had a major impact on American life. But the town's 40-year practice of including a city-owned Nativity display along with secular symbols at the annual Christmas celebrations at Slater Mill Historic Site provoked a significant controversy over the role of religion in public life and government sponsorship of public religious activities.

In 1980 several Pawtucket residents, including ten Protestant clergy, filed suit with the American Civil Liberties Union to challenge the constitutionality of the Nativity display. The clergy persons called a press conference just after Christmas to explain their positions. They said:

> We call upon public officials not to exploit the strong sentiments associated with religious festivals and divide majority from minority. . . .
>
> While the festivities, lights and generations of good will in this season have roots in both religion and secular tradition, the creche is a specifically religious symbol. Our country, while deeply influenced by a Judeo-Christian heritage, is not itself Judeo-Christian, but is pluralistic, consisting of many rich religious traditions and recognizing the value of all.
>
> Government in our country, wisely recognizing the diversity of these traditions, was set up to steer clear of embracing any,

while protecting the religious freedom of all.

We as pastors have a responsibility to educate our people in the history of religious strife and the futility of imposing religious beliefs on the human conscience. The specifically religious observance of this holiday period belongs in our homes, and in our churches and synagogues. Although there are public recognitions of this glad season, they should be confined to those symbols and traditions which are not identified with any one group.

The press conference was called to counteract the actions of the city's mayor, Dennis M. Lynch. Lynch adored Christmas and tried to share that enthusiasm with others. Each year he placed trees, a tinsel-trimmed desk, an office Nativity scene, ribbons, lights and cardboard Santa Clauses in his City Hall office. Outside he arranged Christmas music, peppermint-striped lamp-posts and the creche.

Lynch denied that he did it for religious reasons. He said the decorations symbolized nonsectarian good will. But when the lawsuit was filed, Lynch hit back with a press conference at Slater Mill, where he defiantly led sixty municipal workers in singing Christmas hymns. Then he harangued the crowd, pounding the podium with clenched fists, and declaimed about patriotism, freedom and Christmas.

U.S. District Judge Raymond J. Pettine refused to rule before Christmas, calling the dispute a "serious and delicate question of constitutional law." The highly respected judge, who takes church-state separation seriously, first ruled that the ACLU director Steven Brown did not have standing to bring the suit because he was not a Pawtucket taxpayer. In October 1981, he allowed the civil liberties group to name three city taxpayers as plaintiffs.[3]

On November 10 of that year, in *Donnelly v. Lynch*, he ruled the city-owned Nativity scene unconstitutional, saying that "government may not assist in the fight to keep Christ in Christmas." He also rejected the city's argument that Christmas is a secular holiday in which the Nativity scene has lost its purely religious meaning. Pettine said that "Christmas remains a major spiritual feast for most . . . Christians" and has gained secular significance without losing its religious meaning.[4]

On November 3, 1982, the U.S. First Circuit Court of Appeals issued a permanent injunction against the city of Pawtucket, forbidding government sponsorship of the creche. The city had sold the life-size display of the birth of Jesus to a private group in an attempt to minimize its involvement.[5] Then the U.S. Supreme Court accepted the appeal.

It may be appropriate at this point to look in some detail at that much-used phrase from the First Amendment: "Congress shall make no law respecting an establishment of religion. . . ." This explicit constitutional ban on religious establishment remains at the core of the juridical relationship between religion and government in the United States. Because of heightened sensitivity to the protection, and perhaps because of increasing intersections between church and state during the past half-century, this doctrine has taken on a unique life of its own. Hence, the phrase, "establishment clause doctrine," has become part of our legal language.

The classic definition of what "no establishment" means was written by Justice Hugo L. Black in a 1947 case concerning public support for parochial schools in New Jersey. In that ruling, *Everson v. Board of Education,* Black wrote:

> The "establishment of religion" clause of the First Amendment means at least this: neither the state nor the Federal Government can set up a church. Neither can pass laws which aid one religion, aid all religions, or prefer one religion over another. Neither can force nor influence a person to go or to remain away from church against his will or force him to profess a belief or disbelief in any religion. No person can be punished for entertaining or professing religious beliefs or disbeliefs, for church attendance or nonattendance. No tax in any amount, large or small, can be levied to support any religious activities or

institutions, whatever they may be called, or whatever form they may adopt to teach or practice religion. Neither a state nor the Federal Government can, openly or secretly, participate in the affairs of any religious organizations or groups and vice versa. In the words of Jefferson, the clause against establishment of religion by law was intended to erect "a wall of separation between church and state."[6]

A quarter of a century later, the High Court enunciated a three-part test in *Lemon v. Kurtzman*.[7] To pass constitutional scrutiny, legislation had to have a secular purpose, could not advance or inhibit religion, and could not result in "excessive entanglement" between church and state. It was the *Lemon* test that invalidated many attempts by lawmakers to subsidize church-related elementary and secondary education. And the test has also been applied to many questions surrounding religious activities in public education and disputes involving religious symbolism on public property.

There are other aspects of the establishment doctrine that are relevant. It is a truism to say that the First Amendment prohibited the establishment of any kind of national religion. Justice William O. Douglas noted that, "The First Amendment does not select any one group or any one type of religion for preferred treatment."[8]

The purpose of the adoption of the establishment clause was broad and far-reaching. Justice Wylie Rutledge observed:

The First Amendment's purpose was not to strike merely at the official establishment of a single sect, creed or religion, outlawing only a formal relation such as had prevailed in England and some of the colonies. Necessarily it was to uproot all such relationships. But the object was broader than separating church and state in this narrow sense. It was to create a complete and permanent separation of the spheres of religious activity and civil authority by comprehensively forbidding every form of public aid or support for religion.[9]

Justice Douglas argued that the Founders "fashioned a charter of government which envisaged the widest possible toleration of conflicting [religious] views."[10]

Furthermore, government cannot "suppress real or imagined attacks upon a particular religious doctrine,"[11] nor can it have any "interest in theology or ritual."[12]

Government may not prefer religion or religious persons over those who profess no religion. Justice Hugo L. Black wrote:

> We repeat again and again reaffirm that neither a state nor the Federal Government can constitutionally force a person "to profess a belief or disbelief in any religion." Neither can constitutionally pass laws or impose requirements which aid all religions as against non-believers, and neither can aid those religions based on a belief in the existence of God as against those religions founded on different beliefs.[13]

Government may not "compose official prayers for any group of the American people to recite as part of a religious program carried on by government."[14]

Justice William L. Brennan affirmed, "The State must be steadfastly neutral in all matters of faith, and neither favor nor inhibit religion."[15]

The state may not "require that teaching and learning must be tailored to the principles or prohibitions of any religious sect or dogma,"[16] according to Justice Abe Fortas. In the same case Fortas also observed:

> Government in our democracy, state and national, must be neutral in matters of religious theory, doctrine, and practice. It may not be hostile to any religion or to the advocacy of no religion; and it may not aid, foster, or promote one religion or religious theory against another or even against the militant opposite. The First Amendment mandates governmental neutrality between religion and religion, and between religion and nonreligion.[17]

Churches are "excluded from the affairs of government,"[18] said Chief Justice Warren E. Burger, and "important, discretionary governmental powers" may not be "delegated to or shared with religious institutions."[19]

Government may not "foster a close identification of its powers and responsibilities with those of any or all religious denominations . . . ,"[20] said Justice William J. Brennan. Justice Brennan also noted that it is forbidden for legislation "to employ the symbolic and financial support of government to achieve a religious purpose."[21]

With this background, let us see how the Supreme Court applied establishment clause doctrine to the first creche case.

On March 5, 1984, the High Court ruled that the two lower federal courts were wrong. The city of Pawtucket could include a Nativity scene as part of an official Christmas display without violating the principle of separation of church and state, "notwithstanding the religious significance of the creche."[22]

To reach its decision, Chief Justice Warren Burger, joined by Justices Byron White, Lewis Powell, William Rehnquist and Sandra Day O'Connor, relied heavily on historical practices such as state-paid legislative chaplains, annual days of Thanksgiving, national mottos employing religious language, and inclusion of religious paintings in publicly owned art galleries. Burger noted, "There are countless other illustrations of the government's acknowledgment of our religious heritage and governmental sponsorship of graphic manifestations of the heritage."[23]

The Court held that the city of Pawtucket had "principally taken note of a significant historical religious event long celebrated in the Western World. The creche in the display depicts the historical origins of this traditional event long recognized as a National Holiday."[24]

The Burger Court also seemed to be moving away from the three-prong test that it had established to deal with religion clause cases. In 1971 the Court said in *Lemon v. Kurtzman* that legislation had to be tested for whether its principal or primary effect advanced or inhibited religion, whether it had a secular purpose, and whether it created an excessive entanglement between government and religion. In this case, however, Burger said, "We have repeatedly emphasized our unwillingness to be confined to any single test or criterion in this sensitive area."[25] But Burger went ahead and applied the test to this case and held that the city's action passed muster. Writing for the majority, he said, "We are satisfied that the City has a secular purpose for including the creche, that the City has not impermissibly advanced religion, and that including the creche does not create excessive entanglement between religion and government."[26]

The majority seemed to go out of its way to ridicule those who wanted to adhere to strict separation of church and state. Burger wrote, "In our modern complex society, whose traditions and constitutional underpinnings rest on an encouraged diversity and pluralism in all areas, an absolutist approach in applying the Establishment Clause is simplistic and has been uniformly rejected by the Court."[27] He concluded that the Court wanted to "protect the genuine objectives of the Establishment Clause" but that "it is far too late in the day to impose a crabbed reading of the Clause on the country."[28]

Dismissing the "fears and political problems" of the past which produced the First Amendment, the Chief Justice said, "We are unable to perceive the Archbishop of Canterbury, the Vicar of Rome, or other powerful religious leaders behind every public acknowledgment of the religious heritage long officially recognized by the three constitutional branches of government."[29]

Burger admitted that "the display advances religion in a sense but our precedents plainly contemplate that on occasion some advancement of religion will result from governmental action."[30]

Calling the creche a "passive symbol," Burger argued, "To forbid the use of this one passive symbol—the creche—at the very time that people are taking note of the season with Christmas hymns and carols in public schools and other public places, and while the Congress and Legislatures open sessions with prayers by paid chaplains would be a stilted overreaction contrary to our history and to our holdings. If the presence of the creche in this display violates the Establishment Clause, a host of other forms of taking official note of Christmas, and of our religious heritage, are equally offensive to the Constitution."[31]

Justice Sandra Day O'Connor, the crucial swing vote, argued in a separate concurring opinion, "What is crucial is that a government practice not have the effect of communicating a message of government endorsement or disapproval of religion."[32]

In a strongly worded dissent Justice William Brennan, joined by Justices Thurgood Marshall, Harry Blackmun, and John Paul Stevens, said the majority decision was "contrary to our remarkable and precious religious diversity as a nation."[33] By upholding public sponsorship of a sectarian religious symbol, Justice Brennan said, "The prestige of the government has been conferred on the beliefs associated with the creche."[34] This means, he continued, that "the effect on minority religious groups, as well as those who may reject all religion, is to convey the message that their views are not similarly worthy of public recognition nor entitled to public support. It was precisely this sort of religious chauvinism that the Establishment Clause was intended forever to prohibit."[35]

Justice Brennan, always concerned about the integrity of religion, denied that the creche was a mere representation of an historic event. He maintained:

It is instead best understood as a mystical recreation of an event that lies at the heart of Christian faith. To suggest as the Court does that such a symbol is merely traditional and therefore no different from Santa's house or reindeer is not only offensive to those for whom the creche has profound significance but insulting to those who insist for religious or personal reasons that the story of Christ is in no sense a part of "history" nor an unavoidable element of our national "heritage."[36]

Brennan chided the court majority. "I am convinced," he wrote, "that this case appears hard not because the principles of decision are obscure, but because the Christmas holiday seems too familiar and agreeable. Although the Court's reluctance to disturb a community's chosen method of celebrating such an agreeable holiday is understandable, that cannot justify the Court's departure from controlling precedent."[37]

Brennan also reproved his colleagues for ignoring history. "The American historical experience concerning the public celebration of Christmas, if carefully examined, provides no support for the Court's decision."[38]

Justice Harry Blackmun, in a separate dissent, made these trenchant comments:

> The creche has been relegated to the role of a neutral harbinger of the holiday season, useful for commercial purposes, but devoid of any inherent meaning and incapable of enhancing the religious tenor of a display of which it is an integral part. The city has its victory but it is a Pyrrhic one indeed.
>
> The import of the Court's decision is to encourage use of the creche in a municipally sponsored display, a setting where Christians feel constrained in acknowledging its symbolic meaning and non-Christians feel alienated by its presence. Surely, this is a misuse of a sacred symbol. Because I cannot join the Court in denying either the force of our precedents or the sacred message that is at the core of the creche, I dissent and join Justice Brennan's opinion.[39]

The decision had its vocal supporters. Among them was the Rev. Jerry Falwell, president of the Moral Majority, who said, "This ruling portends good things for the future." Falwell's lieutenant, Cal Thomas, claimed that the court had removed "religious Americans from second-class citizenship."

Monsignor Daniel F. Hoye, general secretary of the United States Catholic Conference, said the ruling "appears to affirm the reasonable view that government can accommodate the interests of the citizens in this matter without doing violence to any Constitutional principles." He added that the Pawtucket decision was in line with the more flexible and realistic approach to church-state relations adopted by the Supreme Court in some other recent rulings—an approach in accord with the Catholic Conference's own thinking in this area."

Many religious and civil liberties groups were disturbed and perplexed by the ruling. The Rev. Dean Kelley, religious liberty specialist for the National Council of Churches, said the Court "regressed from important principles of religious liberty." He continued:

> For the government to sponsor the symbols of one particular religion is to derogate the belongingness of citizens of other faiths or no faith. Further, to take the most sacred symbols of one religious group and desacralize them as just one in a row of secular folk symbols like Santa Claus and Rudolph the Red-Nosed Reindeer is a great loss to the religious groups that view those symbols as sacred.

The nation's Jewish community expressed considerable dismay. Henry Siegman, executive director of the American Jewish Congress, called the decision "troubling for religious minorities." He added, "It should also prove troubling for those concerned with religion, for government endorsement necessarily compromises religious messages."

Norman Redlich, dean of New York University Law School, said the decision sends a message that Jews are "strangers in their own land."

The *Miami Herald*'s Jim Hampton undoubtedly spoke for many when he wrote:

> As one reared in the Christian faith, I fully appreciate the religious significance of Nativity scenes. That's why, as a civil libertarian, I am profoundly distressed by the U.S. Supreme Court's ruling. . . . Government has no more right to help us Christians flaunt our beliefs than it has to suppress any faith. In abandoning that principle, this Court majority has put its desire to be agreeable above its duty to be impartial.[40]

Pawtucket was not the only municipality to be involved in legal challenges of this nature. The village of Scarsdale, a town of 17,000 affluent residents in New York's Westchester County, saw its longstanding controversy reach the High Court in 1985.

Beginning in 1956, at the request of four Scarsdale churches, the village Board of Trustees granted permission to place a creche during the Christmas season at Boniface Circle, a city-owned park located in the center of the business district. The next year, the churches formed the Scarsdale Creche Committee in order to commission and maintain the creche. Each year the Committee submitted a written application to the Board seeking permission to exhibit the creche. In 1960 the Scarsdale chapter of the American Jewish Congress objected formally to the creche but the board dismissed the complaint. The controversy continued to simmer. By 1973 several board members joined citizens in objecting to the display.

In 1976 a local attorney filed suit against the board for allowing the creche, but the challenge was dismissed for lack of subject-matter jurisdiction.[41] That year the board established a Human Relations Advisory Council to offer advice on inter-faith conflicts. In 1979 the board reluctantly granted permission but "strongly recommended that the Creche Committee consider rotating the creche among various village churches in future years." Four of the eleven churches had withdrawn from the Creche Committee because of the divisions the dispute was causing. Five congregations offered to display the creche on their property but the committee was not interested, even though the Community Baptist and Scarsdale Congregational churches were centrally located. A small sign was placed near the creche, indicating that a private organization erected and maintained it.

In 1981 the board had had enough. By a four-to-three vote it denied the Creche Committee's request. That year the creche was displayed at a local restaurant. Mayor Jean Stone, a Christian who displayed a creche at her home, cast the deciding vote. She switched when she was persuaded that ample private property was available. She was also dismayed and shocked by the rising tempo of anti-Semitic letters and phone calls board members were receiving. The creche, she said, is "a solid, seeable religious arti-fact . . . and you see it there in the heart of Scarsdale on village property like the village is supporting it." The local *Scarsdale Inquirer* editorialized that the "community's good will would be better served if the Creche Committee would accept, with grace, the village board's decision and place the creche at an appropriate location. This could be the healing step to avert divisiveness in future years."

Alas, it was not to be. Kathleen McCreary, a lawyer and coordinator of the pro-creche forces, threatened legal action to compel the exhibition. She told an emotion-charged and packed meeting of the board that Christians had the right "to celebrate our personal religious convictions and avail ourselves of our constitutional right of freedom of religious expression."

The room erupted in applause. Sure enough, McCreary and company filed suit in federal district court in 1983, charging that their right of free speech and free exercise of religion had been violated by the board decision. The village lawyer responded that a religious display on public property gave the aura of official government sponsorship or approval, thus violating the First Amendment ban on establishment of religion. The pro-creche forces also cited the "open public forum" argument, which was probably crucial. (Incidentally, the attorneys for both sides were Jewish, which may have been a deliberate attempt to contain some of the undeniable religious prejudice this conflict had engendered.)[42]

A minor complication arose when two groups, the Citizens' Group, and the Scarsdale Creche Committee, each filed suit against the Village of Scarsdale. The District Court consolidated the two actions in June 1983 and a trial was held on July 20 of that year.

On December 8, 1983, the District Court ruled that the village did not have to allow the creche on public property. The court held "it was proper for the village to deny plaintiffs' applications in order to avoid contravening the Establishment Clause."[43]

Proponents of the creche were undeterred. They appealed to the Court of Appeals for the Second Circuit, which ruled in their favor. The appellate court decided that the village could not refuse a private group's request to display a creche in a public park which had traditionally been the site of other religious and secular events. The court held the park to be an open public forum. In that context the display of a creche fell under the protection of the free speech clause.[44]

In March of 1985 a sharply divided Supreme Court agreed with the appellate court in a four-to-four ruling which is limited in its applicability.[45] The decision, however, resolved nothing, leaving Scarsdale officials and their counterparts elsewhere uncertain as to what they should do.

The Supreme Court made a third attempt to resolve the legal complexities surrounding holiday displays on public property when it announced its decision on July 3, 1989, in *County of Allegheny v. ACLU.*[46] A sharply divided Court ruled that a creche located in a county courthouse, which was surrounded by a floral arrangement and a sign proclaiming "Glory to God in the Highest," violated the Establishment Clause, while a county office building display, which consisted of a menorah and a Christmas tree alongside a sign proclaiming "Salute to Liberty," did not have the unconstitutional effect of endorsing the Christian or Jewish faiths.

This litigation began on December 10, 1986, when seven local residents and the Greater Pittsburgh Chapter of the American Civil Liberties Union filed suit in federal district court against Allegheny County and the City of Pittsburgh, seeking permanently to enjoin the county from displaying the creche in the Grand Staircase of the County Courthouse and the city from displaying a menorah in front of the City-County Building. The district court on May 8, 1987, rejected the injunction and held that both displays had a general secular purpose and were only part of the holiday decorations. A divided panel of the Third Circuit Court of Appeals reversed this ruling the following year and declared that both symbols were an unconstitutional endorsement of religion and were located "at or in a public building devoted to core functions of government."[47] A petition for rehearing was denied, and the U.S. Supreme Court chose to review the bitterly contested case.

This complicated and lengthy ruling included multiple opinions, dissents, and concurrences by various justices. Essentially, the justices ruled five-to-four against the creche but six-to-three in favor of the menorah. Their reasoning processes, however tortuous, remain normative at least for the foreseeable future.

Several principles that will guide lower courts in resolving the December dilemma were enunciated in this case. Among them are the following:

1. Celebration of Christmas as a national holiday does not of itself validate the constitutionality of a creche on public property.

2. Although government may acknowledge Christmas as a cultural phenomenon, the Establishment Clause prohibits it from observing Christmas as a Christian holy day.

3. Government may celebrate Christmas in some manner or form, but not in a way that endorses Christian doctrine.

4. Confining the government's celebration to its secular aspects does not favor the religious beliefs of non-Christians over Christians but permits government to acknowledge the holiday without expressing allegiance to Christian beliefs.

5. If a city celebrates Christmas and Hanukkah as religious holidays, it violates the Establishment Clause. Simultaneous endorsement of Judaism and Christianity is no less unconstitutional than endorsement of Christianity alone. But, if a city celebrates both Christmas and Hanukkah as secular holidays, its conduct does not violate the Establishment Clause.

6. The erection of Christmas trees alone does not constitute endorsement of Christian belief.

The swing votes in *Allegheny* came from Justices Blackmun and O'Connor, who agreed that the crucial question in determining the constitutionality of Christmas and Hanukkah decorations is whether or not the government action involved amounts to an endorsement of religion, so that nonadherents are made to feel like outsiders.

Accordingly, Blackmun and O'Connor said it was crucially necessary to examine the context of each display. The unadorned creche in the courthouse, they concluded, gave the unmistakable impression of government endorsement of Christianity. But the menorah and tree display, accompanied by a sign suggesting that these representations validated freedom of religion, were not, taken as a whole, to be seen as endorsements of the two religions. In effect, Blackmun and O'Connor gave another endorsement to the so-called "plastic reindeer rule," the contemptuous term now employed by lawyers who must argue these cases. The less religious the symbol, or the greater number of secular symbols surrounding the religious one, the more likely the exhibit is to pass muster.

Blackmun's creche decision, joined by O'Connor and by the three separationists, Brennan, Marshall and Stevens, held that "the creche itself is capable of communicating a religious message . . ."[48] and "the effect of a creche display turns on its setting."[49] Because of the setting, "The county sends an unmistakable message that it supports and promotes the Christian praise to God that is the creche's religious message."[50]

Defenders of the creche tried to make pivotal the fact that it was accompanied by a sign indicating its ownership by a private Roman Catholic organization, the Holy Name Society. But Blackmun dismissed that saying, "The sign simply demonstrates that the government is endorsing the religious message of that organization."[51]

Rejecting any free-exercise claim, as advanced by the pro-creche lobby in the Scarsdale case a few years before, Blackmun commented, "Christians remain free to display creches in their homes and churches. To be sure, prohibiting the display of a creche in the courthouse deprives Christians of the satisfaction of seeing the government adopt their religious message as their own, but this kind of government affiliation with particular religious messages is precisely what the Establishment Clause precludes."[52]

Justice William Brennan, writing for the waning separationist wing of the Court, criticized the Court's ruling that Hanukkah is a partly secular holiday, thereby rendering its celebration by civil authority more constitutionally acceptable. "The menorah is indisputably a religious symbol, used ritually in a celebration that has deep religious significance."[53] Brennan said, "I cannot accept the effort to transform an emblem of religious faith into an innocuous symbol."[54] Brennan, more than any other justice in recent years, did his homework and explored the history, theology and culture of religious groups before arriving at his carefully crafted opinions. Brennan reminded his colleagues that "The government-sponsored display of the menorah alongside a Christmas tree works a distortion of the Jewish religious calendar,"[55] because, as he noted, Hanukkah is a relatively minor Jewish holiday that has been elevated in United States life only because of its proximity to Christmas. Thus, the drift of this and other recent Court rulings, Brennan said, "has the effect of promoting a Christianized version of Judaism."[56] Brennan's fundamental concern for the integrity of religious belief has seldom been more eloquently expressed than in this dissent.

Brennan also criticized the kind of pluralism supposedly endorsed by the Court's decision. "The holiday calendar they appear willing to accept revolves exclusively around a Christian holiday. Those religions that have no holiday at all during the period between Thanksgiving and New Year's Day will not benefit, even in a second-class manner, from the city's once-a-year tribute to 'liberty' and 'freedom of belief.' This is not pluralism as I understand it."[57] Finally, Brennan strongly chided the Court's attempt to define pluralism:

The uncritical acceptance of a message of religious pluralism also ignores the extent to which even that message may offend. Many religious faiths are hostile to each other, and, indeed, refuse even to participate in ecumenical services designed to demonstrate the very pluralism Justices Blackmun and O'Connor extol. To lump the ritual objects and holidays of religions together without regard to their attitudes towards such inclusiveness, or to decide which religions should be excluded because of the possibility of offense, is not a benign or beneficent celebration of pluralism: it is instead an interference in religious matters precluded by the Establishment Clause.[58]

In another dissent Justice John Paul Stevens said, "The Establishment Clause should be construed to create a strong presumption against the display of religious symbols on public property because there is always a risk that such symbols will offend nonmembers of the faith being advertised as well as adherents who consider the particular advertisement disrespectful."[59]

Stevens also raised an interesting point: the objection that many Christians have to government's attempts to preempt Christian symbols. He wrote, "Some devout Christians believe that the creche should be placed only in reverential settings, such as a church or private home."[60] In a footnote Stevens cited the *amicus* brief filed by the National Council of Churches in this case, which argued that "government acceptance of a creche on public property . . . secularizes and degrades a sacred symbol of Christianity."[61]

Even the Court's conservative wing was displeased with aspects of the ruling, since they wanted to sustain both creches and menorahs as part of their drive to strengthen accommodation and to weaken the Court's adherence to a strict interpretation of the Establishment Clause. Justice Anthony Kennedy lobbied for a new and much limited test for the establishment of religion. Government actions, to be rendered unconstitutional, had to "coerce individuals to support or participate in any religion or its exercise."[62] Direct benefits that tend to create a state religion or to proselytize on behalf of a particular religion should be invalidated. "Passive and symbolic" acts of recognition or accommodation of religion or "intangible benefits" to religion are acceptable in Kennedy's view. (Ironically, Kennedy proved to be the crucial vote in striking down school-sponsored prayers at public school graduation exercises in the *Lee* v. *Weisman* decision in 1992.)

Kennedy and his allies concluded that "the creche and menorah are purely passive symbols of religious holidays."[63] Kennedy's dissent in the creche portion of the *Allegheny* decision accused his colleagues of "trivializing constitutional adjudication" and "embracing a jurisprudence of minutiae."[64] His frustration, however understandable, ignored the fact that it was the conservative majority in *Lynch* five years before which constructed the plastic reindeer rule and inaugurated a decade of artistic hair-splitting worthy of medieval theology's angels on a needle.

The importance of this case and the degree of division on the Court was immediately evident when the decision was announced on July 3, 1989. Justice Kennedy accused Blackmun of "latent hostility," "callous indifference," and "unjustified hostility toward religion." Blackmun responded that "Nothing could be further from the truth," adding, "These accusations could be said to be as offensive as they are absurd."[65]

Reaction to the decision varied from mildly critical to hostile, except from the Lubavitchers, an ultra-Orthodox Jewish group, also called Chabad, who have been promoting these activities for a decade. Most Jewish groups were displeased with the split decision. Henry Siegman, executive director of the American Jewish Congress, said, "We are unhappy that the Court strained to give the menorah a secular meaning. In a sense this denudes the menorah of its truly religious significance." On the right, the National Legal Foundation executive director Robert K. Skolrood accused the Court of being "manipulated by antireligious fanatics out to destroy the beliefs and cherished values that made our nation strong." Neoconservative gadfly Michael Novak said the ruling "made me feel like an outsider in my own country . . . it seems that the less religious a symbol, the more acceptable it is to the new secular orthodoxy."[66]

The *Louisville Courier-Journal* had this to say about the *Allegheny* case in its July 5, 1989, editorial: "No amount of packaging can disguise the religious meaning of a Nativity scene, menorah or other religious symbol. What has gotten lost is the principle that the freedom of all faiths, and non-faiths, is best protected when government does not give its blessings to any."

A number of appellate court decisions have continued to fine-tune the legal doctrines pertaining to the permissibility of religious symbols on public property.

Even before the Supreme Court's *Allegheny* decision, the Sixth Circuit on June 11, 1986, held that a city-owned Nativity scene on the front lawn of the Birmingham, Michigan, City Hall violated the ban on Establishment of Religion. The appeals court affirmed a federal district court's ruling that a publicly-financed religious symbol standing alone on public property violated all three prongs of the Establishment Clause test formulated by the Supreme Court in the 1971 *Lemon v. Kurtzman* case.[67]

The appeals court concluded that the Birmingham creche had the impermissible effect of advancing Christianity, because the effect of the display was to call attention "to a single aspect of the Christmas holiday—its religious origin. A creche standing alone without any of the nonreligious symbols of Christmas affirms the most fundamental of Christian beliefs, that the birth of Jesus was not just another historical event." The Court concluded, "It is difficult to believe that the city's practice of displaying an unadorned creche on the City Hall lawn would not convey to a non-Christian a message that the city endorses Christianity."

This court also made a valuable observation on the nature of our Constitution: "Since the majority does not need its protections, the Bill of Rights was adopted for the benefit and protection of minorities."

The Supreme Court refused to accept the appeal in this case, thus indirectly affirming its decision.[68]

A bitter dispute in Chicago resulted in a major Seventh Circuit ruling in 1987. This case, brought by several Jewish organizations as well as individual Christian and Jewish taxpayers, resulted in a temporary victory for supporters of a long-time Nativity display at the Chicago City Hall.

The district court in *American Jewish Congress v. City of Chicago* found the creche matched "squarely the Christmas context contemplated by the Supreme Court in *Lynch v. Donnelly*." Furthermore, said the court, "The entire display sponsored by the city is to celebrate a national holiday with a secular purpose not negated by the inclusion in the display of a traditional symbol of that holiday, the Nativity scene."[69]

The Chicago case had several interesting antecedents. Since about 1948 a creche had been displayed in the City Hall lobby. A few secular symbols were also displayed on various city properties. In 1978 a suit was filed seeking to enjoin the city from expending public funds for the erection and maintenance of creches in City Hall and Water Tower Park. The consent decree entered in that case stipulated that no public funds could any longer be used, and that any creche erected through private means must display a disclaimer of government endorsement.[70]

The city of Chicago transferred ownership of the creche to a private organization, the Chicago Plasterers Institute. A few years later an eight-foot free-standing menorah was erected in Daley Center Plaza. (Opposition to the menorah was originally a part of the complaint in this case but it was dropped, with leave of court.)

Politics then entered the picture. On December 7, 1984, Mayor Harold Washington ordered the creche dismantled. But negative public opinion prompted the Chicago City Council Finance Committee to pass a resolution calling for re-erection of the creche. The mayor's enemies saw this as a gift on a silver platter. Four days later the creche was reassembled. The next year, despite objections from many citizens, the City Council passed a resolution endorsing the public display of the creche and the menorah.

The Court's ruling was noteworthy because of the rhetoric

of Judge Frank J. McGarr. McGarr's decision rivaled those of Alabama's Brevard Hand, whose frequently overruled decisions have suggested that states may establish their own religion and can remove textbooks which allegedly espouse "secular humanism" from public schools. Judge McGarr stopped just short of saying the United States was a Christian nation where non-Christian minorities are merely tolerated.

McGarr concluded that America's origins were Christian, that its founders had "intended and achieved full religious freedom for all within the context of a Christian nation in the First Amendment as it was adopted, rather than as we have rewritten it."[71] He also complained about "the erroneous view of the First Amendment which has brought us where we are."[72]

This court's ruling attacked the thrust of modern Supreme Court doctrine in the church-state arena. Judge McGarr also made an egregious error when he asserted that compulsory chapel services exist at the three service academies. They were, in fact, struck down as an establishment violation by a federal court in a 1972 decision, *Anderson v. Laird.*

Judge McGarr also held the creche to be "a mere seasonal tradition, pleasant in its associations and connotations and no longer necessarily religious."[73]

An appeal was filed before the Seventh Circuit Court of Appeals on February 20, 1987, and a three-judge panel heard arguments in the case in May of that year. The Seventh Circuit, as expected, overruled Judge McGarr's decision on August 18, 1987. In a two-to-one decision the appellate court ruled that placement of a religious tableau in a government building "inevitably creates a clear and strong impression that the local government tacitly endorses Christianity" and "unavoidably fosters the inappropriate identification of the City of Chicago with Christianity."

Writing for the appellate court majority, Judge Joel Flaum said that locating a Nativity scene in City Hall sends a powerful symbolic message. He observed:

Like the Nativity scene itself, City Hall is a symbol—a symbol of government power. The very phrase "City Hall" is commonly used as a metaphor for government. A creche in City Hall thus brings together church and state in a manner that unmistakably suggests their alliance. The display at issue in this case advanced religion by sending a message to the people of Chicago that the city approved of Christianity.

The court drew this distinction between the Chicago controversy and the *Lynch* one:

The creche in *Lynch*, although sponsored by the City of Pawtucket, was located in a privately owned park, a setting devoid of the government's presence. But the display in this case was located within a government building, a setting where the presence of government is pervasive and inescapable.[74]

Another Illinois case involved the illumination of a Latin Cross on a volunteer fire station's communication tower in the town of St. Charles. From 1970 until a district court's decision in 1985, the cross was part of the city's Christmas display.[75] Other public buildings were decorated with secular symbols. The court found the cross to be an Establishment Clause violation since "a cross on a building has come to have a religious meaning in our society separate from any religious holiday."[76] The primary effect," the court said, "of including an illuminated cross in the city's annual Christmas display is to place the government's imprimatur on the particular religious beliefs associated with the Latin Cross."[77] The court also noted the strange inappropriateness of crosses at Christmas. The cross is, after all, a symbol of the crucifixion and has never been a Christmas symbol. "Unlike the creche, a cross on a building, even during the Christmas season, does not ordinarily conjure up in a viewer's mind the historical antecedents of the Christmas holiday," the court held.[78]

A few months later the Seventh Circuit Court of Appeals affirmed this ruling.[79] The appellate court said the prominent display of a cross "dramatically conveys a message of governmental support of Christianity."[80]

In a major surprise, the Seventh Circuit reversed the logic of several of its own decisions when, in 1989, it allowed a Chicago suburb to maintain a creche on the lawn of its town hall. The Seventh Circuit reversed a district court decision which had barred the practice two years before. This court also issued a *per curiam* order, did not hear arguments on the factual merits of the case, and chose to grant summary disposition.[81] It is decisions like this one which leave legal scholars and local officials baffled.

The placement of a menorah in City Hall Park in Burlington, Vermont, came to the attention of the Second Circuit in 1989 after the Vermont District Court dismissed the complaints of those who challenged the city's permission to allow the Lubavitch group to erect the menorah.[82] The Second Circuit reversed that ruling and held that an unattended, solitary display of a menorah in a public park adjacent to city hall violated the Establishment Clause. The menorah, the court held, was clearly a religious symbol and was displayed alone so that there was nothing to indicate that the thrust of its message was secular rather than religious.[83] The court majority also suggested that religious divisiveness would be reduced when "emotion-laden religious symbols" are reserved to places of worship and in homes rather than on public property.[84] The court also disagreed with the U.S. Supreme Court on two points. It said, "The menorah, like the creche, is clearly a religious symbol."[85] The court also held that not all public fora, such as parks, are acceptable places for religious symbols. "The existence of a public forum is simply a factor to be taken into account in determining whether the context of a display suggests government endorsement."[86]

The Second Circuit reaffirmed this decision in a case involving the same parties and with a slightly different fact situation in *Chabad-Lubavitch of Vermont v. City of Burlington.*[87]

Another 1989 ruling, this one from the Eighth Circuit, dealt with the tricky case of a menorah display, complete with daily religious ceremonies, on the Iowa state capitol grounds. In 1986 Rabbi Moishe Kasowitz was given permission by the state's director of general services to erect a menorah and to hold worship services each day. However, an attorney general's opinion caused the permission to be revoked a few days later. The motion for a preliminary injunction was denied.[88] The state argued that it had a reasonable right to forbid the erection of permanent religious symbols on state property.

This case was complicated by the fact that Christmas trees were present in the capitol rotunda and on the state house grounds. State-owned trees were decorated with angels. Another state-owned tree had secular decorations. This caused one district judge to dissent from the initial ruling preventing the menorah. He argued, "The state is obligated to treat all religions evenhandedly. So long as Christian symbols are permitted, other religions should be given equal treatment."[89] The angels were removed from the tree in 1987.

The district court held that no constitutional violation existed when the state refused to permit the menorah display. There was no discrimination because all religious organizations were forbidden to erect permanent religious displays.[90] This decision was affirmed by the Eighth Circuit on May 8, 1989.[91]

In the following year four appellate court decisions were rendered. The Fourth Circuit upheld a district court ruling[92] that a Nativity scene erected by the Jaycees on the front lawn of the Albemarle County, Virginia, Office Building violated the Establishment Clause despite a relatively small disclaimer as to the source of sponsorship.

The Fourth Circuit reasoned that even though the lawn was a public forum, a creche not associated with any secular symbols or artifacts and located in a prominent place in front of an important government structure constituted official endorsement. The court also held that there was a compelling state interest in removing any suggestion of government endorsement of religion.[93]

The Fourth Circuit rejected the argument that a sign disclaiming government involvement was an acceptable way of avoiding the appearance of establishment. "The unmistakable message conveyed is one of government endorsement of religion impermissible under the Establishment Clause of the Constitution. The endorsement of the religious message proceeds as much from the religious display itself as from the identification of a religious sponsor."[94]

This case, originating in Thomas Jefferson's home town of Charlottesville, revealed intense divisions within the religious community. The plaintiffs included six Christian and Unitarian ministers, a rabbi, and three private individuals of varied religious backgrounds. The defendants, the Albemarle County Board of Supervisors, were joined by a number of evangelical and fundamentalist churches and pastors.

The Sixth Circuit decided two Christmas cases in 1990. One, *ACLU v. Wilkinson*,[95] was issued on the same day as *Smith v. Albemarle*. This circuit reached different conclusions when it held that a Nativity scene on the Kentucky Capitol grounds *would not* amount to an endorsement of Christianity by the state of Kentucky if it were accompanied by a prominent and clearly worded sign disclaiming all state involvement. This decision upheld a district court ruling[96] which held that the Nativity scene could remain on the capitol grounds if a sign disclaiming government involvement was erected in a prominent place. The court even suggested the proper wording to be used: "This display does not constitute an endorsement by the Commonwealth of any religion or religious doctrine."[97]

The Kentucky case had a couple of unusual twists. The Kentucky state capitol complex, housing the offices of the governor, attorney general, the General Assembly, and the Supreme Court, was decorated by considerable Christmas paraphernalia, including evergreen strands, red bows, white lights, red ribbons, wreaths, and a lighted Christmas tree. About a hundred yards away a stable, 15 feet high, with a floor area of 30 feet by 20 feet, was erected. A corral adjoined the stable. Both were constructed by state government employees at a cost of $2,400 in

1988. The stable was first used on November 28th of that year when a Catholic school staged a live Nativity pageant there. Two additional programs were presented before a group of plaintiffs filed a complaint.

Though the activities were clearly religious in nature, the district court found the area was "a recognized public forum."[98]

Later in the year the Sixth Circuit rendered a decision in *Doe* v. *City of Clawson*.[99] This time the court concluded that the display of a creche on the lawn of a city hall in Clawson, Michigan, contained sufficient secular symbols to convey a message of pluralism. Therefore, the creche's appearance, even though it implied the support and approval of the civil authorities, did not violate the First Amendment's prohibition on government endorsement of religion.

The dispositive factor seems to have been the court's belief that the creche was "sufficiently adorned with secular symbols so as not to convey a message of government endorsement of religion."[100] The plaintiffs in this case had argued that the Nativity scene dominated the Christmas holiday season display, but the court rejected that contention.

The Sixth Circuit took pains to claim that this decision was not a departure from their ruling in the Birmingham case, where an unadorned creche was considered an unconstitutional endorsement of Christianity. The endorsement analysis was the key. In this case the creche "is displayed in the context of the Christmas holiday season."[101] The Clawson display had fewer secular symbols than in Pawtucket, but it had enough to satisfy the Sixth Circuit.

On November 6, 1990, the Seventh Circuit upheld a district court decision which concluded that menorahs do not have to be allowed at Chicago's O'Hare Airport but that Christmas trees and garlands were acceptable because they are not religious symbols. This case, *Lubavitch Chabad House, Inc.* v. *City of Chicago*,[102] issued three major points of law.

1. "The City's display of Christmas trees with decorations at the airport, while refusing to allow menorahs, did not constitute religious discrimination or an equal protection violation."[103]

2. "Christmas trees standing alone or among other secular symbols of Christmas are without religious connotation.[104] The current jurisprudence regarding the secular nature of Christmas trees is further buttressed by the historical origins of Christmas trees. Most authorities on the subject agree that the use of greenery in general and Christmas trees in particular are derived from ancient pagan customs."[105]

3. "The city's regulation of all free-standing religious symbols in public areas is valid as a reasonable time, place or manner restriction because it is content neutral."[106]

On May 15, 1992, the Seventh Circuit issued a ruling in a case that had bounced back and forth for two years. This complicated case dealt mainly with the question of religious paintings in a public park in the town of Ottawa, Illinois.

In 1956 the Ottawa Retail Merchants Association commissioned the painting of sixteen scenes from the life of Christ in an effort to "put Christ back in Christmas." These paintings were displayed at the Christmas season in Washington Park from 1957 to 1969 and again from 1980 through 1988. The park in question had a long history as a public forum, and was the site of one of the Lincoln-Douglas debates in 1858. The City of Ottawa arranged for the erection of the paintings from 1964 to 1967, but private organizations exhibited them during the other years. During the 1970s the exhibition had been discontinued, and the paintings were stored under an old grandstand and apparently forgotten. After the city parks superintendent discovered them in 1980, the local chapter of the Jaycees, a national service organization, decided to become the caretakers and exhibitors of these works of art.

In November of 1986 a local resident, Richard Rohrer, objected to the exhibition as an endorsement of Christianity, but the

Ottawa City Council adopted a resolution supporting the exhibition as part of a "cooperative effort by the community to provide appropriate seasonal yuletide spirit." Two years later Rohrer filed a complaint with the federal district court seeking to enjoin the display. The complaint was amended after Rohrer moved away from Ottawa, and a Jane Doe was substituted as plaintiff on June 12, 1989.

The district court held the display unconstitutional under the Establishment Clause.[107]

On appeal the Seventh Circuit affirmed this ruling,[108] but a rehearing *en banc* was granted[109] (en banc means that the entire panel of the Seventh Circuit participated in the decision, not the usual three-member panel).

This time the appeals court reversed its own ruling. This ruling[110] held that the previous ruling was "overbroad" because it restrained the speech of parties not party to the suit. Furthermore, the city could not exclude private persons from the park merely because of the religious content of their speech. In addition, the court ruled, the mere presence of religious symbols in a public forum does not violate the Establishment Clause, since government is not presumed to endorse every speaker. However, the fact situation "may require removal of religious displays if there is no other narrowly tailored manner of avoiding the appearance of governmental endorsement of the message."[111]

This case attracted considerable outside interest. Pat Robertson's National Legal Foundation was an intervenor-appellant on the city's side. The American Jewish Congress and the Anti-Defamation League of B'nai B'rith filed *amicus curiae* briefs for the plaintiff, urging that the initial decisions be reaffirmed.

The Seventh Circuit held that "the overbroad injunction was a content-based exclusion of speech without a compelling state interest to support it."[112]

This case's outcome clearly hinged on the free speech and public forum concepts enunciated in the Scarsdale case and in such cases as *Widmar v. Vincent.*[113] But even in a concurring opinion Judge Cudahy warned that "a private religious group may so dominate a public forum that a formal policy of equal access degenerates into endorsement."[114] Also, he noted, "Surely the city cannot allow a religious group to turn a public park into an enormous outdoor church."[115]

The Sixth Circuit returned to this issue in November 1992, which in another *en banc* hearing ruled nine-to-six that the erection of a menorah in Calder Plaza in Grand Rapids, Michigan, during the eight days of Hanukkah was not unconstitutional.

The display had been privately funded since 1984, and the city had no role in the planning, erection, removal, maintenance or storage of the menorah. In 1990 several local taxpayers, led by longtime civil liberties activist and attorney Albert Dilley, filed suit in federal district court to enjoin the city from allowing the display. A preliminary injunction was granted but the Sixth Circuit stayed the injunction.[116] On March 21, 1991, the district ruled that this display violated the Constitution, and both Chabad House and the city appealed to the Sixth Circuit. A panel of the Sixth Circuit affirmed the district court ruling.[117] However, on June 25, 1992, the full court vacated the panel's decision and granted a rehearing.

The sharply divided court chose to rely solely on the free speech and equal access cases, as they had done in a previous menorah case from Cincinnati the year before.[118] They concluded, ". . . we hold that truly private religious expression in a truly public forum cannot be seen as endorsement by a reasonable observer."[119]

Judge Pierce Lively issued a stinging dissent in which he concluded:

> The fact that religious expression takes place in a public forum does not in any way lessen the force of the Establishment Clause. . . . Every unit of government in the United States, including the City of Grand Rapids, has a compelling interest in observing the Establishment Clause and preserving the values that Clause guarantees. To accept the majority's construction of the interplay between Establishment Clause principles and

the public forum doctrine would turn the Establishment Clause into a paper screen rather than the bulwark of separation between church and state it was intended to be.[120]

Echoing Justice Brennan's dissent in *Allegheny*, Judge Lively also argued that "displays of this kind inevitably have a greater tendency to emphasize sincere and deeply felt differences among individuals than to achieve an ecumenical goal. The Establishment Clause does not allow public bodies to foment such disagreement."[121]

The most recent appellate court decision in a creche case was announced by the Ninth Circuit on March 3, 1993. It was a complex ruling which still leaves open several disputed questions.

The case, *Kreisner v. City of San Diego*,[122] involves one of the oldest and most elaborate Christmas displays in the country, which has been erected in San Diego's Balboa Park since 1953. Balboa Park is a 1,200 acre public facility containing theaters, museums, a zoo, and picnic areas. Every year during the Christmas season, the Community Christmas Center Committee, usually called the Christmas Committee, sponsors a secular holiday display, including Santa Claus, reindeer, a Christmas tree, and lights. That display was not challenged in this case.

What was challenged by taxpayer Howard T. Kreisner and others was a thoroughly religious exhibition at an amphitheater called the Organ Pavilion, located 250 ft. away from the secular display. For a six week period from late November to early January, eight scenes from the life of Jesus, housed in a palm-covered booth, are presented. Each contains a life-size statuary, a painted backdrop, a descriptive sign and Gospel passages in English and Spanish. Disclaimer signs, stating that the biblical display is privately sponsored, accompany the display.

This religious exhibit had in the past been more closely tied to civil authorities. From 1953 to 1988 city employees erected and removed it and stored the scenes on city property, though the statuary and booths were owned by the Committee. A city attorney's opinion in 1988 that such entanglement rendered the city's involvement unconstitutional led to some divestment. The Committee now erects, removes, and maintains the display, and stores it on private property. The Committee reimburses the city $150 for the cost of electricity. These facts appear to have convinced the Ninth Circuit majority that city involvement was minimal.

The city also waived its normal fee for use of the Organ Pavilion. A sliding scale of costs is generally applied to potential users of the park, depending on the nature of the use and the character of the user. Nonprofit organizations that "are of a service or character building nature or who give service to the community" may be excluded from payment requirements, according to city regulations. Consequently, the Christmas Committee has never paid for its participation and seems to have acquired an exclusive access to the park. The city loses $18,000 annually by waiving the normal fee.

By a two-to-one majority, the Ninth Circuit, in an opinion written by Judge Diarmuid F. O'Scannlain, held that "the city may permit the religious display provided it does so in a non-discriminatory manner."[123] O'Scannlain spelled out how he and Judge Alex Kozinski saw this case: "This appeal [from the U.S. District Court for the Southern District of California, CV-88-1993] squarely presents a conflict between two of our most deeply cherished liberties: freedom of speech and freedom of religion."[124]

The court held that the city may permit a private group to erect a religious display in a public park during the Christmas season if the park is a traditional public forum removed from the seat of government.

It was, thus, a fairly narrow ruling that would not apply in many instances, though staunch church-state separationists and religious libertarians, including the dissenting judge, Robert Boochever, could cite this as another slide down a slippery slope toward majoritarianism and state-approved religious insensitivity.

The court majority placed great emphasis on Balboa Park's

experience as a "traditional" public forum.[125] They were also persuaded that a disclaimer sign, "while not dispositive, reinforces the reasonable observer's perception of no government sponsorship."[126]

The Ninth Circuit majority claimed to be expressing concern for and protection of religious authenticity in their ruling. They wrote, "In the same way that government-crafted prayers threaten to water down religious messages, permitting only those Christmas displays that are of minimal 'intensity' will detract from or destroy their religious significance."[127]

The court concluded, further, that the city had a "legitimate, sincere, secular purpose" in promoting a "holiday spirit" and "free expression."[128]

This decision, in some respects, moves judicial doctrine even further toward government accommodation of religion, since it allows an overtly religious display on public property if the sponsors are private and the location is a traditional public forum sufficiently removed from the seat of government. The U.S. Supreme Court has not gone this far, and it is uncertain at this writing whether the city of San Diego will choose to appeal this ruling.

The Ninth Circuit also remanded this case to the district court to make some additional factual findings relative to the use of permits, and to allegations that the city preferred the Christmas Committee's requests over those of competing groups. The essential ruling on the constitutional questions remains undisturbed.

Judge Robert Boochever dissented in the strongest and most compelling manner. He based his dissent on a conviction that "the religious intensity of the display's message is unprecedented,"[129] that the display contains "potent religious imagery," a "quite literal religious message, unaccompanied by any secular symbols."[130] These symbols, he felt, were "blatant, denominational and conspicuous."[131] The display itself was "large and enduring."[132] Therefore, he found the display violated the Establishment Clause because of the nature of the government's involvement.

Boochever noted, "Considering the intensity of the religious message, virtually any government association with the Christmas Committee display would break with the principles announced in the Establishment Clause."[133]

Furthermore, "Any remaining doubts of an Establishment Clause violation were shattered when one considers the city's exemption of the Christmas Committee display from its fee regulations and antisolicitation ordinance."[134]

Judge Boochever was outraged that the Christmas Committee was permitted to place donation barrels and fliers soliciting contributions at its display, while other groups were prohibited from doing likewise.[135]

A number of district courts have also addressed these thorny issues during the past decade.

A federal district court ruled that the state of Mississippi could not illuminate a cross on a state office building or any other state-owned building. For seven years the state had created the image of a Latin cross on the Walter Sillers Building in downtown Jackson, the state capital. The lighted windows formed the shape of a cross extending the full height and breadth of the twenty-story building, which could be seen for miles.

The cross had been the only symbol originally, but bells, a Christmas tree, and the words "Joy" and "Peace" were added, supposedly to give it a more secular cast. The cost of the illumination was borne primarily by the state.

The court held that the display had no secular purpose and, additionally, had the effect of advancing religion. The later inclusion of secular Christmas symbols did not convince the court that the practice passed muster.[136]

A Connecticut District Court in 1985 struck down an illuminated cross from the Cos Cob volunteer fire department. The cross had been part of the building's Christmas display for 30 years. After first determining that a voluntary fire department was a "state actor," the court held that the state and its agents are barred from taking any action that violates the Establishment Clause. Then it proceeded to determine that displaying the cross violated the secular purpose requirement. The court rejected the firemen's contention that the cross became a secular symbol because of the "light and color" it added to the display. The cross had a religious connection with Christmas, said the court.[137]

In 1977, Madalyn Murray O'Hair sought an injunction to remove a Nativity scene from the Texas Capitol rotunda, but federal judge Jack Roberts ruled that Christmas has become so largely a secular holiday that its religious symbolism on public property did not violate separation of church and state. The United States Supreme Court refused to reverse this ruling on October 5, 1981.[138]

A federal court in New Hampshire anticipated the Birmingham, Michigan, decision when it ruled in 1984 that the City of Nashua could not continue its Nativity scene display standing alone in the City Hall Plaza. The court said, "To reasonable persons . . . the display of the creche indicates that the municipal government of Nashua believes that the Trinitarian theory of Christianity is a favored religious doctrine."[139] (The court did suggest that disclaimer of ownership or inclusion of secular symbols might render the exhibit constitutionally acceptable.)

An Illinois district court denied the Lubavitchers their request to erect religious displays in Chicago's Daley Center Plaza even though "the city could not constitutionally prohibit the erection of all religious exhibitions during the December holiday season"[140] and even though Daley Plaza is considered a public forum.

The court also held that placement of Christmas trees, wreaths, and garlands in airport terminals constituted secular expressions of Christmas. However, the court ruled, "In broadcasting music in the proximity of the Christmas trees, recordings of secular Christmas holiday music must be substituted for recordings of strictly religious music."[141]

This is the first court ruling which regulated the content of Christmas music in a public place, opting for the secular over the religious. Courts have now become arbiters of aesthetic taste in their efforts to find constitutionally permissible ways of allowing public Christmas celebrations.

In 1990 a Georgia district court allowed the state to prohibit a menorah in front of the state capitol building on the grounds that this was a noncontent-related policy falling under the "reasonable time, place and manner" restrictions regulating speech in public areas.[142]

In Los Angeles in 1978 a state court disallowed a cross illuminated on city office buildings during Christmastide.[143]

The New York Supreme Court upheld a creche on public property, but that decision was rendered a decade before the U.S. Supreme Court's three-part test for establishment case law.[144]

What may be the most confusing creche case on record occurred in Colorado. This story began when a group of Denver residents calling themselves "Citizens Concerned for Separation of Church and State" sued the city and county on November 28, 1979, to force removal of the creche from the front steps of the Denver City and County Building. Eight days before Christmas, U.S. District Judge Richard Matsch ruled that the state and local government's forty-year-old custom of purchasing, maintaining, erecting and displaying the Nativity scene on government property was unconstitutional. He gave government authorities two days to take it down. But on December 18 the Tenth Circuit Court of Appeals stayed the ruling indefinitely, in order to rule on the merits of the case. The plaintiffs then sought help from U.S. Supreme Court Justice Byron White, who referred the request to the full court. On January 21, 1980, the High Court by a seven-to-two vote, with Justices William Brennan and Thurgood Marshall dissenting, refused to reverse the Appeals Court ruling.

Then almost a year later, on December 4, 1981, U.S. District Judge David K. Winder ruled in favor of the creche. "The message conveyed is not an endorsement by the City of Denver of the Christian faith but rather one of the general celebration of the holiday season," said Winder. He held the Nativity scene to be part of holiday folklore, adding, "It is both a religious symbol of the birth of Christ and a sign of the holiday season on a par with Santa and Mistletoe. Its meaning derives from the context of its use and from the eye of the beholder."

Then in 1982 the Colorado Court of Appeals asked the state supreme court to hear the case again "because the subject matter . . . has a significant public interest and involves legal principles of major significance in the interpretation of the Colorado Constitution."

The state supreme court in 1982 remanded the case to a trial court after determining that the plaintiffs had established a *prima facie* case that the primary effect of the creche display was to advance Christianity.

But the trial court held the creche to be no more than a traditional symbol of a season of good will, not an attempt by government authorities to advance a particular religious faith. The Colorado Supreme Court in September of 1986 ruled that the inclusion of a creche does not violate the "preference" clause (Article 2, Section 4) of the Colorado Constitution. Colorado's highest court concluded that the main purpose of including the creche within a larger holiday display was "to promote a feeling of good will, to depict what is commonly thought to be the historical origins of a national holiday, and to contribute to Denver's reputation as a city of lights."[145]

The city of West Miami, Florida, entered into a consent agreement in 1983 which stipulated that private rather than public funds were to be used for the City Hall creche.[146] In 1966 a Dade County Circuit Court okayed a privately-funded Christmas cross on the Dade County Courthouse. In 1965 a Unitarian minister, John Papandrew, had protested the seven-year-old practice before the county commission.[147]

A Vermont court in 1987 ordered the removal of a lighted cross on top of a Christmas tree in the village of Hyde Park. Judge Jerome Niedermeier concluded, "The cross in the context of Christmas has the effect, at best unintended, of conveying a message of governmental endorsement of Christianity."[148]

Most state and federal courts have refused to allow the erection of crosses on public property on a permanent basis.[149]

Not all of the Christmas-related controversies make it to the courts. Some are decided at city councils, while others are settled by the mere threats of lawsuits.[150]

In 1992 the borough of Manville, New Jersey, removed a creche from the town square after the ACLU of New Jersey threatened legal action against the forty-year-old practice. The year before the ACLU had sued the borough of Rutherford, which forestalled further legal action by moving their creche onto private property. Manville's mayor Angelo Corradino suggested that his town would take the same route.

The Washington, D.C., suburban community of Vienna, Virginia, was sued successfully in 1991 by the ACLU for allowing a local Knights of Columbus chapter to erect an unattended creche at the town's community center. An unattended creche is considered equivalent to government sponsorship and is thus not allowed.

Town officials were so concerned about sparking another lawsuit that they banned religious music from the annual holiday pageant in 1992. This so angered many residents that the Vienna Choral Society withdrew from the program. Two hundred local residents, including fifteen clergy, protested the action by erecting a Nativity scene at the Vienna Community Center on December 6 and defiantly singing religious carols.[151]

Authorities in Fairfield, Connecticut, adopted rules to govern Nativity scenes on public property after local resident Nello Ceccarelli set up a creche on the Town Hall Green in December 1988. The new ordinance required that someone had to remain with the creche at all times.[152] Some city officials are defiant. Mayor John Letts of Naugatuck, Connecticut, said he would go to jail rather than remove a creche from the town green.[153] In Sparta, New Jersey, the town council voted three-to-two against erecting a menorah but allowed a Christmas tree, while Cincinnati allowed a Christmas display in a public park after secular figures were added to a creche.[154]

Some city officials are clearly worried. Bethlehem, Pennsylvania's mayor Ken Smith openly pleaded that his "Christmas City" should be exempt from the drift of recent court rulings because of the town's historic nature and its founding by Moravian immigrants on Christmas Eve in 1742. Secular items were in fact added to the city-owned creche in 1989 to head off any potential legal action.[155]

A number of city officials resent the cost of defending dubious political decisions and of appealing unfavorable court actions. Pittsburgh Mayor Sophie Masloff, noting that her city had spent $150,000 on the *Allegheny* case, arranged for Christmas trees and menorahs to be placed on private property in 1989. Some city council members tried to force the displays into more prominent places but the feisty mayor responded, "I don't think it is worth $150,000 to have a tree and menorah on one side of Grant Street rather than the other."[156] City officials in Charlottesville, Virginia, had to pay $62,000 in legal fees in their appeal of the *Smith* v. *Albemarle* case.[157]

Notes

1.Clement Miles, *Christmas in Ritual and Tradition, Christian and Pagan* (London: T. Fisher Unwin, 1912), pp. 105–107.

2. Francis X. Weiser, *Handbook of Christian Feasts and Customs* (New York: Harcourt, Brace, 1958), p. 94.

3. Albert J. Menendez, "Christmas, Creches and the Courts," *Church & State* 35 (December 1982): pp. 12–15.

4. 525 F. Supp. 1150 (Rhode Island 1981).

5. *Church & State* 35 (January 1982), p. 14. Affirmed 691 F, 2d 1029 (1st Circuit 1982).

6. 330 U.S. 15, 16.

7. 403 U.S. 602.

8. *United States* v. *Ballard*, 322 U.S. 86, 87 (1944).

9. *Everson* v. *Board of Education*, 330 U.S. 31, 32 (1947).

10. 322 U.S. 87.

11. *Burstyn* v. *Wilson*, 343 U.S. 495.

12. *McGowan* v. *Maryland*, 366 U.S. 563, 564 (1961).

13. *Torcaso* v. *Watkins*, 367 U.S. 495 (1961).

14. *Engel* v. *Vitale*, 370 U.S. 425 (1962).

15. *Abington School District* v. *Schempp*, 374 U.S. 226, 229, (1963).
16. *Epperson* v. *Arkansas*, 393 U.S. 106 (1968).
17. 393 U.S. 103, 104.
18. *Lemon* v. *Kurtzman*, 403 U.S. 602, 625, (1975).
19. *Larkin* v. *Grendel's Den*, 459 U.S. 127 (1982).
20. *Grand Rapids School District* v. *Ball*, 473 U.S. 373 (1985).
21. *Edwards* v. *Aguillard*, 107 S.Ct. 2573 (1987).
22. 465 US 668 at 685.
23. Ibid.
24. Ibid. at 682.
25. Ibid. at 69.
26. Ibid. at 685.
27. Ibid.
28. Ibid.
29. Ibid. at 686.
30. Ibid.
31. Ibid.
32. Ibid. at 692.
33. Ibid. at 694.
34. Ibid.
35. Ibid.
36. Ibid.
37. Ibid.
38. Ibid. at 718.
39. Ibid. at 727.
40. Albert J. Menendez, "How the Supreme Court Stole Christmas," *Church & State* 37 (April 1984): pp. 9–10.
41. *Rubin* v. *Village of Scarsdale* 440 F Supp 607 (S.D.N.Y. 1976 (and *Russell* v. *Town of Mamaroneck*, 440 F Supp 607 (S.D.N.Y. 1977).
42. Jim Buie, "Why Christmas Isn't Merry in Scarsdale," *Church & State* 37 (December 1984): pp. 4–5.
43. *McCreary* v. *Stone*, 575 F Supp 1112 9 (S.D.N.Y. 1983).
44. 739 F.2d 716 (2d Circuit 1984).
45. *Board of Trustees* v. *McCreary*, 105 S.Ct. 1859 (1985), 471 US 83.
46. 109 S. Ct. 3086 (1989).
47. 842 F. 2d 655, 662.
48. 109 S. Ct. 3086 (1989) at 3103.

49. Ibid.
50. Ibid. at 3104.
51. Ibid. at 3105.
52. Ibid. at 3105, n. 51.
53. Ibid. at 3127.
54. Ibid. at 3127, 3128.
55. Ibid. at 3128.
56. Ibid. at 3129.
57. Ibid. at 3129.
58. Ibid. at 3128.
59. Ibid. at 3131.
60. Ibid.
61. Ibid. at 3131, n. 8.
62. Ibid. at 3137.
63. Ibid. at 3139.
64. Ibid. at 3144.
65. *Voice of Reason* 30 (Summer 1989): p. 4.
66. Quoted in *Voice of Reason* 30 (Summer 1989): p. 4.
67. *American Civil Liberties Union* v. *City of Birmingham* 791 F 2d 1561 (6th Circuit 1986).
68. 7 *Religious Freedom Reporter* 287–289. 4 *Religious Freedom Reporter* 262.
69. No. 85 9471 (E.D. Illinois, Nov. 5, 1986) at 16.
70. *DeSpain* v. *City of Chicago* 78 c 4997.
71. 7 *Religious Freedom Reporter* 347.
72. No. 85C 9471 (E.D. Illinois, Nov. 5, 1986) at 11.
73. Ibid., at 12–13.
74. *American Jewish Congress* v. *City of Chicago*, 827 F.2d 120 (7th Cir. 1987).
75. *American Civil Liberties Union of Illinois* v. *City of St. Charles*, No. 85-C-09917 (N.D. Illinois, Dec. 5, 1985).
76. 6 *Religious Freedom Reporter* 42.
77. Ibid.
78. Ibid.
79. 794 F. 2d 265, cert. den., 107 S. Ct. 458.
80. 6 *Religious Freedom Reporter* 354.
81. *Mather* v. *Village of Mundelein*, 869 F. 2d. 356 (7th Cir. 1989).
82. 700 F. Supp. 1315.

83. *Kaplan* v. *City of Burlington*, 891 F. 2d 1024 (1989) cert. den., 110 S. Ct. 2619 (1990).

84. Ibid. at 1031.

85. Ibid. at 1028.

86. Ibid. at 1029.

87. 936 F. 2d 109 (2d Cir. 1991), cert. den., 112 S. Ct. 3026 (1992).

88. 808 F. 2d 657.

89. 684 F. Supp. 610, 615.

90. 684 F. Supp. 610 (S.D. Iowa).

91. 873 F. 2d. 1161.

92. 699 F. Supp. 549.

93. *Smith* v. *County of Albemarle*, VA 895 F. 2d 953 (4th Cir. 1990).

94. Ibid. at 958.

95. 895 F. 2d 1098 (6th Cir. 1990).

96. 701 F. Supp. 1296.

97. Ibid. at 1099.

98. Ibid. at 1101.

99. 915 F. 2d 244 (6th Cir. 1990).

100. Ibid. at 246.

101. Ibid. at 248.

102. 917 F. 2d 341.

103. Ibid. at 348.

104. Ibid. at 345.

105. Ibid. at 344.

106. Ibid. at 348.

107. *Doe* v. *Small*, 726 F. Supp. 713 (N.D. ILL 1989).

108. 934 F. 2d 743.

109. 947 F. 2d 256.

110. 964 F. 2d 611 (7th Cir. 1992).

111. Ibid. at 612.

112. Ibid. at 622.

113. 454 U.S. 263.

114. Ibid. at 625.

115. Ibid.

116. *Americans United* v. *City of Grand Rapids*, 922 F. 2d 303 (6th Cir. 1990).

117. 1992 WL 77643, 6th Cir. April 21, 1992.

118. *Congregation Lubavitch v. City of Cincinnati,* 923 F. 2d 458 (6th Cir. 1991).

119. 1992 WL 330327, *14 (6th Cir. Mich.).

120. WL 330327, *28 (6th Cir. Mich.).

121. Ibid.

122. 988 F. 2d 883. (9th Cir. 1993)

123. 1993 U.S. App. LEXIS 3428, p. 2.

124. Ibid.

125. 1993 U.S. App. LEXIS 3428, p. 12.

126. Ibid.

127. 1993 U.S. App. LEXIS 3428, p. 8.

128. 1993 U.S. App. LEXIS 3428, p. 9.

129. 1993 U.S. App. LEXIS 3428, p. 29.

130. 1993 U.S. App. LEXIS 3428, p. 30.

131. Ibid.

132. Ibid.

133. Ibid.

134. 1993 U.S. App. LEXIS 3428, p. 31.

135. For an overview, see Mary C. Nixon, "Christmas Sojourn in San Diego," in *Christmas: The Annual of Christmas Literature and Art,* vol. 56 (Minneapolis: Augsburg Publishing House, 1986), pp. 50–54.

136. *American Civil Liberties Union v. Mississippi State General Services Administration,* 652 F. Supp. 380 (1987).

137. 6 *Religious Freedom Reporter* 85–86 (*Liben v. Town of Greenwich,* No. B84-805 (D. Conn., Dec. 10, 1985).

138. *Church & State,* 35 (December 1982), p. 12.

139. *Barelle v. City of Nashua* 599 F. Supp. 792 (D. New Hampshire, 1984).

140. *Grutzmacher v. Public Building Commission,* 700 F. Supp. 1497 (N.D. Ill., 1988).

141. Ibid. at 1504.

142. *Chabad Lubavitch of Georgia v.Harris,* 752 F. Supp. 1063 (N.D. Ga., 1990).

143. *Fox v. City of Los Angeles,* 22 Cal. 3d 792, 587 P 2d 663 (1978).

144. *Lawrence v. Buchmueller,* 40 Misc. 2d 300, 243 NYS 2d 87 (NY Sup. Ct. 1963).

145. *Conrad v. City and County of Denver,* No. 84SA 313 (Colo. Sept. 8, 1986). See also 6 *Religious Freedom Reporter* 13; 1 *Religious*

Freedom Reporter 10, 141, 171. See *Conrad v. City and County of Denver*, 656 P 2d 662 and *Citizens Concerned v. Denver*, 526 F. Supp. 1310 (D. Colo. 1981).

146. "Tinsel and Trouble," *Church & State* 36 (February 1983): p. 11.

147. *Paul v. Dade County*, 202 So 2d 833 (Fla. Dist. Ct. App.) cert. denied 207 So. 2d 69 (Fla. 1967).

148. *Church & State* 41 (January 1988), p. 3. The case was *White v. Village of Hyde Park*.

149. *American Civil Liberties Union v. Rabun County Chamber of Commerce*, 698 F. 2d 1098 (11th Cir. 1983); *Lowe v. City of Eugene*, 254 Or 518,, 463 P 2d 360 (1969) cert. denied 397 US 1042 (1970); and *Eugene Sand & Gravel Inc. v. City of Eugene*, 276 Or 1007, 558 P 2d 338 (1976), cert. denied, 434 US 876 (1977).

150. Dawn Onley, "Nativity Scene Banished," *Courier-News* (December 30, 1992).

151. Maria Koklanaris, "Ministers Beseech Vienna," *The Washington Times*, December 24, 1992.

152. *Church & State* 42 (June 1989): p. 22.

153. *Church & State* 43 (February 1990): p. 39.

154. *Church & State* 42 (November 1989): p. 16.

155. *Church & State* 43 (December 1990): p. 18.

156. *Church & State* 44 (January 1991): p. 18.

157. *Church & State* 43 (December 1990): p. 18.

8

Religious Symbols
and the Public Square

The ambiguity of court rulings at several levels of the judicial system has given little concrete guidance to local officials. Groups on both sides of the great church-state divide continue to press their interpretations of these decisions. Community sensitivity varies, but even the most religiously pluralistic areas are not immune from the disputes. The political culture, a changing Supreme Court, commercial interests, the ubiquity of Christmas celebrations, trends in interfaith marriages, and convergence between religious groups will all contribute to a possible resolution of the conflict. (It is also possible that no resolution will ever be found, and that the present stalemate will perdure for the foreseeable future.)

The Jewish community remains divided on the issue of Christmas, though most Jewish Americans clearly oppose tax-supported religious symbols on public property. For Jews, religion is much rooted in private celebrations and the family context.

The issue is complicated somewhat because an estimated 40 percent of Jews are married to Christians, and many celebrate Christmas. Some observe a secular Christmas, while others observe Hanukkah. Still others observe both holidays. Many Jews enjoy the Christmas season. It was, after all, Irving Berlin who wrote the most popular seasonal song of all time, "White Christmas."

Jews are not alone in finding compromises with the season. Native Americans have blended indigenous religious customs with Christmas solemnities for a century.

Francis E. Leupp, the U.S. Commissioner of Indian Affairs, surveyed Christmas activities throughout Native American communities in 1906 and found a considerable intermingling of ancient tribal customs with Christian traditions brought by missionaries and teachers. The Northern Cheyenne, he reported, refer to Christmas as "Big Sunday," while the Arapahoes called it "the birthday of the son of the stranger on high." Many of the customs he labeled "decidedly picturesque." Leupp's patronizing tone, however, mars his portrait. Referring to the San Felipe Indians in New Mexico, for example, he claimed, "Like most primitive people, they make an odd jumble of things Christian and pagan."[1]

These cultural admixtures have been preserved most abundantly among the Zuni Pueblo Indians of New Mexico. At least nineteen pueblos in the Rio Grande Valley continue a centuries-old tradition that links Pueblo beliefs with those of Hispanic Christianity. This is a cross-cultural pageant, occurring each December, and attracting visitors from far and wide.[2]

There is evidence of a conservative backlash over this issue. Religious Right groups see the Christmas creche controversy as part and parcel of a substantive clash over the broader issue of religious symbols on public property. In their view the annual creche controversy is part of a larger struggle over how much the majority religious culture to which they adhere may press its symbolic claims on the entire society. Adhering essentially to a narrow version of Christmas, they promote a narrow vision of society's responsibility to promote equality for religious minorities, at the symbolic levels.

These Religious Right pressure groups now encourage communities to maintain religiously oriented Christmas pageants.

Rightwing legal pressure groups have arisen to challenge the litigation agenda of the American Civil Liberties Union, the American Jewish Congress, and other groups. One of the leaders is the American Center for Law and Justice (ACLJ), a branch of Pat Robertson's Regent University in Virginia Beach, Virginia. In 1992 the ACLJ sent letters to all of the nation's 15,500 public school districts to press them to implement the Equal Access Act, passed by Congress and signed by President Reagan in 1984. They have sought to interpret that act in ways that many critics say goes beyond the clear intent of Congress. The ACLJ lobbies for student-initiated religious expression in music and class reports and favors the establishment of extracurricular Bible clubs. They continue to seek expansion of the public forum concept. The ACLJ's chief counsel, Jay Sekulow, advocates greater accommodation between church and state, between religious groups and local political and educational authorities.

Sekulow's letter, which was also sent to 18,000 mayors and public officials around the country, claimed that "certain national groups have been pressuring local school districts to censor any religious observance of Christmas, when court decisions permit these holiday observances."[3] The ACLU's Washington legislative counsel, Robert Peck, criticized Sekulow's letter as "full of misrepresentations and errors" and citing Supreme Court opinions "out of context."[4]

This offensive impinges on the Christmas controversy. The ACLJ caused the Clark County Nevada School District to overrule a ban on religious music at the Vegas Verdes Elementary School's winter pageant in December 1992.[5]

The clash over the proper boundaries of free speech, or more specifically religious free speech, particularly as it pertains to the protection of religious minorities, is likely to increase during the 1990s.

The bitterness surrounding this issue seems unrelenting. Columnist John Leo wrote angrily of the ACLU's "creche squad": "The yuletide work of the American Civil Liberties Union is never done. While others frolic, the grinches of the ACLU tirelessly trudge out each year on yet another creche patrol, snatching Nativity scenes from public parks and rubbing out religious symbols."[6] Leo's sarcasm knows no end. Accusing religious libertarians of "running off to judges to get every trace of religion extinguished from public life," Leo charges that "many Christians feel that the state is taking an increasingly active role in erasing the religious Christmas and inflating the secular one."[7] Leo also criticizes the "evasive arguments and reindeer-ridden Supreme Court decisions," and urges the "tedious anticreche zealots to end their crusade."[8]

Leo seems oblivious to the role that government plays when it encourages public observances of religious events, or places itself in the position of advancing one religious position over others. The annual Christmas controversies may be tedious, and less than civil in discourse, but they involve fundamental principles of American life and law.

An even stronger broadside was leveled by a new ultraconservative magazine calling itself *Dimensions*, which in a cover story in its December 1992 issue accused the Supreme Court of "waging war on Christmas." The magazine cover featured an original painting depicting the Court's justices firing a cannon at Santa Claus.

Public opinion seems to favor the construction of Nativity scenes on public property, or at least finds them insufficiently threatening to good communal and interfaith relationships.

A 1987–1988 survey conducted by the Center for Communication Dynamics at George Washington University in Washington, D.C., found 80 percent of respondents agreeing that "It's ok for a city government to put up a manger scene on government property." Only 13 percent disagreed and 7 percent did not have an opinion. Sharp differences were noted among those polled. Support was somewhat lower among those under age twenty-two, government officials, and those in the media. College professors were opposed by 54 percent to 37 percent. The most pronounced differences were found among the clergy. While 88 percent of Catholic priests and 85 percent of Protestant ministers were favorable to publicly sponsored creches, only 14 percent of the rabbis supported them.

A related question about menorahs also elicited 79 percent support, 15 percent opposition, and 7 percent without opinions. This question was phrased, "It's ok for a city government to put up candles on government property for a Jewish celebration." The results were broadly similar to the creche question, though 5 percent of Protestant clergy favored nativity scenes but opposed menorahs.[9]

Two additional polls, conducted by the Survey Research Center of the University of Kentucky in December 1988 and November 1989, found similarly high levels of support. In 1988, 82 percent of Kentuckians favored erection of a Nativity scene on the grounds of the state capitol in Frankfort. The 1989 survey found 81 percent of residents in favor of retaining the creche. Only about 10 percent of residents opposed Governor Wallace Wilkinson's decision to erect the scene and even to allow it to be used by church groups for fullscale pageants.

James Hougland of the University of Kentucky assessed the poll's findings and concluded, "Support for the Nativity scene was relatively common among older, conservative, nonurban residents, but it also spilled over into relatively well-educated respondents and those with higher income."[10] Only city dwellers, Democrats and political liberals showed lower support for the creche. Hougland added that the creche had a "following that is not confined to the demographic categories that traditionally support conservative religious positions."[11]

This survey, one of the very few conducted on the issue, may have implications far beyond the Bluegrass State.

Another survey, conducted in January 1989 by the Louisville *Courier-Journal* not only found only 7 percent opposed to the creche, but discovered that voters did not perceive the issue in church-state terms. Only 36 percent of those polled thought the creche issue involved separation of church and state.[12]

Hougland's interpretation of Kentuckians's response is insightful. He writes, "While it is probably true that most Americans do not want the government to interfere in religion, citizens of areas with strong religious traditions and a relative scarcity of adherents of non-Christian faiths apparently have trouble translating abstract ideas about church-state separation into implications for actual practices involving familiar symbols."[13]

This recognition of hostile public opinion should by no means deter church-state separationists from pursuing the issue of public sponsorship of religious symbols. Public opinion on the issue of school prayer has also been hostile to the U.S. Supreme Court's rulings striking down mandated prayers and Bible readings in public schools. For thirty years voters have either failed to understand what the Court did in 1962 and 1963 or they have consistently continued to reject that posture. This has not prevented civil libertarians and separationists from continuing to press the implementation and enforcement of the ban, and they should not be expected to give up the fight over religious symbols either. It is a certainty that religious conservatives and church-state accommodationists will maintain their aggressive activities on these fronts for the foreseeable future.

The importance society attaches to Christmas can be seen in a child custody and divorce case in Ohio. In *Pater* v. *Pater*[14] a court granted custody of children to a Roman Catholic father and prohibited the children's mother, a Jehovah's Witness, from sharing her religious beliefs with her children during their visitation periods. Testimony from "expert witnesses" emphasized that Jehovah's Witnesses do not celebrate Christmas and that the children might somehow be harmed when they observe their mother's religious-based indifference to the holiday. However, the Ohio Supreme Court[15] reversed the decision, ruling that it would not harm the children if their mother did not celebrate Christmas with them.

A 1991 Gallup Poll gives some insights into the way Americans relate to Christmas. Commercial, familial and charitable aspects of the holiday clearly transcend the purely religious. Eighty-five percent of Americans surveyed have Christmas trees at home, 78 percent send Christmas cards, and 77 percent help the less fortunate during the season. A majority say they attend Christmas parties, sing carols, and generally enjoy the holiday season.

As to religion, some interesting facts emerged. While three persons in four say they celebrate Christmas in a religious way, only 38 percent consider Christmas a "strongly religious holiday." Of those polled, 36 percent said they attend church on Christmas Eve and 25 percent attend on Christmas Day. (Some may attend both times.) Interestingly, of those who bought Christmas stamps, 53 percent preferred the secular while 47 percent chose the religious-themed stamps.

In general terms, 90 percent of Americans celebrate Christmas, 4 percent celebrate Christmas and Hanukkah, 1 percent celebrate only Hanukkah, and 5 percent celebrate neither holiday. Since about 8 percent of Americans have no religious affiliation and 32 percent are not members of a church or synagogue, many millions of U.S. residents must celebrate Christmas as a primarily secular occasion.[16]

This survey corroborates the importance of Christmas to American life, and underscores both the prominence of the legal battles and the difficulty church-state separationists will have in challenging many of the public activities legally. Of course, the findings also underscore the secularity of the holiday for many people.

As previously mentioned, a number of Christian churches still refuse to accept Christmas as a special day of worship or celebration. America's 858,000 Jehovah's Witnesses recognize no holy days, nor do they even acknowledge their own birthdays. The Armenian Apostolic Church, one of the world's oldest Christian communities, observes the Nativity as part of its Epiphany festival, which was the practice when the Armenian Church was established.

The Christian Scientists have no service on Christmas Day, unless it falls on a Sunday, when the regularly appointed Lesson Topic is followed. This American-founded denomination observes only Thanksgiving Day as a holy day. Its founder, Mary Baker

Eddy, promulgated a series of twenty-six Lesson Topics, consisting of scripture readings and passages from her book *Science and Health with Key to the Scriptures*, to be used twice a year.

One of the Lesson Topics is "Christ Jesus" which is often used in December, though not necessarily each year. The Christian Science Hymnal includes "O Little Town of Bethlehem," "Joy to the World," "It Came Upon the Midnight Clear," and a John Greenleaf Whittier poem, "Let Every Creature Hail the Morn." It also includes a setting of Mrs. Eddy's 1898 Christmas poem, "Christmas Morn."

Christian Science authorities, at the First Church of Christ, Scientist in Boston (the Mother Church), have not entirely forgotten Christmas, however. The church's Board of Directors decided in 1949 to publish all of Mrs. Eddy's essays, sermons and messages on the "true significance of Christmas." This tiny volume, called *What Christmas Means to Me and Other Christmas Messages*, is still in print.

Mrs. Eddy denies the doctrine of the Incarnation and opts for a completely spiritualized, or what she calls "incorporeal" view of the Nativity.

Though the Christian Science Church refuses to count its members as a matter of conviction, some estimates place the church's adherents at 300,000 in the United States.

The highly independent Churches of Christ, who claim 1,683,000 members in 13,134 congregations across the nation, have no official policy regarding Christmas worship services or observances. Historically, this conservative group, arising out of the Campbellite movement in early-nineteenth-century America, frowned on Christmas as being biblically unwarranted. But today more and more congregations are holding Christmas services, according to a well informed pastor, Steve Keller, of Rockville, Maryland. Keller said that about 20 percent of Church of Christ congregations, especially those in metropolitan areas, hold Christmas services, and the number is growing each year. Christmas carols and hymns are included in the hymnals commonly used.[17]

The convergence of majoritarian religion and majoritarian

government has never been a happy experience for religious minorities. Neither has it led to harmonious relationships among religious groups, nor to the kind of productive cohesiveness that builds solidarity and unity among disparate peoples.

The United States is a unique society, multicultural, multiracial, and multireligious. Unlike the former Yugoslavia, the myriad of peoples who have together created and sustained this federal Union have chosen to live together and to respect profound differences in culture and religion. We have not achieved perfection, and our historical record has been marred from time to time by nativist, exclusivist outbursts and frenzy. Nevertheless, we have taken giant strides toward the creation of a human family, within which all members, even the least among them, are cherished and wanted.

Religious conservatives often plead for a more open public square, alleging, often erroneously, that the public square is somehow barren or bereft of diversity. In actual fact, the public square is quite diverse and even cluttered with options which the rest of the world can only envy.

True access to the public square is dependent upon respect for minority viewpoints and the preservation of the principle of separation of church and state. Without these historic and constitutionally mandated protections, the public square would likely be closed to many.

The historical record of intolerance in the United States by many of the powerful conservative religious groups gives one pause in contemplating their sincerity in advocating a more open public square. It remains a matter of public record that religious conservatives in the past wanted a closed public square and did their best, when they exercised political and legal power, to repress diversity and to exclude others, primarily Catholics, Jews, humanists, and religious liberals, from full participation in public life.

The issue of Christmas celebrations under public auspices is an integral part of the entire issue of religious symbolism in the public square. Are symbolic issues substantive? Some would argue that symbols matter little. They belong to the penumbrae of these issues and are not central to the debate over the proper role of religion in public life. Others argue that symbolism is everything; it goes to the heart of what a nation and a people are all about. Symbolic issues are on the cutting edge of the never-ending debate over separation of church and state.

In the past decade, the tragic abdication of the Supreme Court as guarantor and protector of religious minorities can only be seen as a lamentable and deplorable trend that should be reversed.

This drift away from full protection of religious minorities by the nation's highest court is directly attributable to the appointments of Presidents Ronald Reagan and George Bush, who promised political allies among the nation's right wing religious organizations that they would appoint justices who supported a larger public role for religious groups and enterprises.

What this has accomplished is a return to majoritarian religious power at the expense of America's many religious minorities. This shift toward greater accommodation of religious pressure groups now threatens American pluralism precisely at a time when pluralism has become a central fact of life in this century's final decade. This redefinition of the role of religion in public life has come simultaneously on three fronts.

As the Establishment Clause has been steadily eroded, the protection traditionally accorded to religious minorities is in jeopardy. The Establishment Clause protects all religious and philosophical positions and their adherents, creates a level playing field and insures an open public square for the expression of opinion.

Gregg Ivers, assistant professor of government at the American University in Washington, D.C., addresses these issues in his timely book, *Redefining the First Freedom*. He interprets the political implications of the decline of Establishment Clause guarantees in this way: "Politically powerful religious groups have been successful in seeking public funds from government to support their private education and social welfare work, all of which promotes majoritarian religious values. But smaller religions and unpopular faiths, unable to persuade majoritarian bodies, lose in the Rehnquist Court."[18]

But the free exercise of religion clause of the First Amendment has also been seriously jeopardized by the Supreme Court's five-to-four ruling in an Oregon case affecting the religious rights of Native Americans.[19] The author of that decision, Justice Antonin Scalia, even suggested that religious freedom may have become a "luxury" that Americans can no longer afford! Ivers regards this ruling as a devastating loss for religious liberty and tolerance. He writes, "Freedom of religion, once considered sacrosanct among the fundamental freedoms entitled to vigorous judicial protection against majoritarian rule, enters the 1990s relegated to the unaccustomed and unforeseen position of second-class stature in our constellation of constitutional values. The historical evolution of the First Amendment free exercise clause in the modern judicial era had breathed real life into the parchment promise of religious freedom for religious minorities, and further strengthened the rights of all individuals to believe and practice their religious beliefs free from government intrusion. But the preferred position of religious rights under the Constitution has vanished. The *Smith* decision demolishes the constitutional protection that, for the better part of four decades, had shielded unorthodox religious conduct from the legislative will of intolerant majorities. This result is not simply unfortunate; it is tragic."[20]

Small religions, and those that are traditionally unprepared for political intrigues, are clearly at a disadvantage in the new climate of church-state jurisprudence. So are those who reject organized religion or who eschew participation in religious activities. Politically marginal and less well organized religious bodies are clearly burdened by their inability to compete with the larger, more politically powerful, religious groups which increasingly dominate life in the United States. The long-term resolution of constitutional issues affecting the religious options of all Americans will clearly be affected by the forces at work throughout the judicial system. In that area, at least, the legacy of the Reagan-Bush era will extend into future decades, since these two former presidents appointed more than two-thirds of the present federal judiciary.

In case after case during the 1980s, the United States Supreme Court ruled either in favor of popular or well known religious groups or in favor of the state when disfavored religious minorities were involved.

This bring us finally to the symbolic issue of religion in the public domain. The symbolic issues are, at once, the most subtle and the most insidious of the many departures from established doctrine and precedent long thought inviolable.

Ivers expresses a concern shared by many.

> Government endorsement of religion in the public sphere presents a quandary that goes directly to the heart of what the establishment clause was designed to prevent: government preference for religious values over nonreligious values and privileges accorded to one religion over others. . . . Government-sponsored religious displays, although displayed seasonally, nonetheless put forth a clear message that some religions are officially recognized and preferred above all others. . . .[21]
>
> Government support for Nativity scenes and menorahs signals the citizens identifying with neither that certain beliefs deserve official recognition, endorsement, and celebration, and that others do not.[22]

In the final analysis, these trends can only lead to serious conflict between church and state in America's future. Both religious integrity and constitutional freedoms are weakened. In the mad rush to accommodate religious majorities, the federal courts are increasingly denuding religious symbols of all inherent values, thereby leading, ironically, to a greater secularization of the sacred. Already, we have seen that Nativity scenes and Christmas trees are increasingly seen as religiously neutral or irrelevant, as memories or traces of religious sentiment. So, too, are menorahs, despite strong historic evidence to the contrary.

The courts have even moved toward secularizing Good Friday, a day in the Christian calendar which simply has no secular counterpart or significance. In April 1991, the Ninth Circuit upheld a Hawaii district court ruling four years earlier which concluded that a Hawaii law granting a paid holiday to government workers on Good Friday was not unconstitutional. The lower court held that Hawaii's legislature had merely intended to give hard-working government employees a "needed day off from work" which could be used for religious or secular purposes.[23] Incredibly, the Ninth Circuit agreed and held that even though the statute "accommodated the widespread religious practices of its citizenry," it was "nothing more . . . than an extra day of rest for a weary public labor force."[24]

The thrust of these decisions clearly suggests a clouded future for the survival of a free conscience, the right of dissent, and that ancient but rarely achieved goal of a free church in a free state. Professor Ivers is right when he observes, "The preferred status that the Supreme Court has conferred upon sectarian religion in the civic culture communicates a disturbing message about the place of religious minorities in American public life."[25]

Even as conservative a jurist as Justice Anthony Kennedy shares these concerns. In his majority opinion in Lee v. Weisman, Kennedy wrote, "A state-created orthodoxy puts at grave risk that freedom of belief and conscience which are the sole assurance that religious faith is real, not imposed."[26]

Notes

1. Francis E. Leupp, "How the Indians Spend Christmas," Ladies Home Journal 24 (December 1906). Reprinted in Philip Reed Rulon, Keeping Christmas: The Celebration of an American Holiday (Hamden, Conn.: Archon Books, 1990), pp. 151–59.

2. William Clark, "Pueblo Winter Dances," New Mexico Magazine 70 (December 1992), pp. 8–9. See also Bobbi Salinas-Norman, Indo-Hispanic Folk Art Traditions (Oakland, Calif.: Pinata Publications, 1992).

3. Larry Witham, "Christian Group Fights Under Free-Speech Flag," *Washington Times*, December 22, 1992, p. A3.

4. Ibid.

5. Ibid.

6. John Leo, "A Secular Christmas to All!" *U.S. News & World Report*, December 28, 1992, p. 31.

7. Ibid.

8. Ibid.

9. The Williamsburg Charter Survey on Religion and Public Life, issued on February 3, 1988.

10. James G. Houghland, Jr., "The State and Observances of Religious Holiday Traditions: Attitudes toward Nativity Scenes on Government Property," *Sociological Analysis* 53, no. 3 (1992): pp. 299–308.

11. Ibid., at 306.

12. Dick Kaukas, "Most Think Judge Erred in Creche Case," Louisville *Courier-Journal*, February 5, 1989, p. A1.

13. Hougland, p. 307.

14. 63 Ohio St. 3d, 588 N.E. 2d 794 (1992).

15. Ibid., at 800.

16. Robert Bezilla, ed. *Religion in America 1992–1993* (Princeton: Princeton Religion Research Center, 1993), pp. 46–47.

17. Telephone interview with Pastor Keller, March 17, 1993.

18. Gregg Ivers, *Redefining the First Freedom* (New Brunswick, N.J.: Transaction Publishers, 1993), p. 95.

19. *Employment Division of Oregon v. Smith*, 110 S.Ct. 1595 (1990).

20. Ivers, pp. 172–73.

21. Ibid., p. 126.

22. Ibid., p. 127.

23. *Cammack v. Waihee*, 673 F. Supp. 1524 (D. Hawaii, 1987).

24. *Cammack v. Waihee*, 932 F.2d. 765, 777 (9th Cir. 1991). cert. denied, 112 S. Ct. 3027 (1992).

25. Ivers, p. 127.

26. *Lee v. Weisman*, 112 S.Ct. 2649, 2657, 2658 (1992).

Index

165

Druids, 31, 36

Eastern Churches, 35
Egeria, 24
Eisenhower, Dwight, 68–70, 76
Ephem the Syrian, 19
Epiphanias, 16, 17
Epiphany, 12, 13, 17, 19, 20
Ericson, Edward L., 76
Establishment Clause, 160
Establishment doctrine, 110–13
Establishment of Religion, 101,
   102
Ethelred, 33
Evelyn, John, 46, 47

Falwell, Rev. Jerry, 116
Feldheim, Rabbi Edward H., 97
Flaum, Judge Joel, 128
Florey v. Sioux Falls, 96
Foley, Daniel J., 57
Ford, Gerald, 70, 72
Fortas, Justice Abe, 112
Francis of Assisi, St., 107

Gallup Poll, 156, 157
Good Friday, 163
Gosse, Edmund, 50
Gregory I, Pope, 35
Gregory III, Pope, 107
Gregory of Nazianzus, 21
Gregory the Wonderworker, St.,
   17
Gross, Leonard, 86
Gundhar, 33

Haakon the Good, 33
Hampton, Jim, 117

Hanukkah, 72, 74, 88, 94, 97, 99,
   100, 102, 152
Harbaugh, Rev. Henry, 58
Harding, Fred F., 84
Harding, Warren, 66
Harrison, Benjamin, 65
Hawaii, 61, 62
Helena, St., 20
Herbs, 35–37
Hillary of Poitiers, St., 32
Hippolytus, St., 16, 17
Holiday Extension Act of 1875, 50
Holly, 36, 37
Holy Family, Feast of the, 23
Holy Innocents, Feast of the, 23
Holy Name Society, 122
Honorius, 20
Hoover, Herbert, 66
Hougland, James, 155, 156
Hoye, Monsignor Daniel F., 116

Ivers, Gregg, 160–63
Ivy, 37

Jehovah's Witnesses, 156, 157
Jews and Christmas, 84–88, 97,
   100, 117–20, 151–52
John Chrysostom, St., 17
John the Evangelist, St., 23
Johnson, Lee, 100
Johnson, Lyndon, 70, 71
Julius I, Pope, 18
Justinian, 20, 24

Kainen, Ruth Cole, 60, 61
Kalends, 28, 29, 33
Karas, Sheryl Ann, 31, 34
Kasowitz, Rabbi Moishe, 131